Religious Pieces
in
Prose and Verse.

Early English Text Society.
Original Series, *No.* 26.
1867, 1914 (*for* 1913).
Price 5s.

Religious Pieces

in

Prose and Verse.

EDITED FROM ROBERT THORNTON'S MS. (Cir. 1440)

IN THE LINCOLN CATHEDRAL LIBRARY,

BY

GEORGE G. PERRY, M.A.,

PREBENDARY OF LINCOLN AND RECTOR OF WADDINGTON,
EDITOR OF *Morte Arthure*.

[*Re-collated with the MS., enlarged and revised* 1913.]

GREENWOOD PRESS, PUBLISHERS
NEW YORK

OXFORD
UNIVERSITY PRESS

Great Clarendon Street, Oxford OX2 6DP
United Kingdom

Oxford University Press is a department of the University of Oxford.
It furthers the University's objective of excellence in research, scholarship,
and education by publishing worldwide. Oxford is a registered trade mark of
Oxford University Press in the UK and in certain other countries

© The Early English Text Society 2006

The moral rights of the authors have been asserted

Database right Oxford University Press (maker)

First Edition published in paperback 2006

All rights reserved. No part of this publication may be reproduced,
stored in a retrieval system, or transmitted, in any form or by any means,
without the prior permission in writing of Oxford University Press,
or as expressly permitted by law, or under terms agreed with the appropriate
reprographics rights organization. Enquiries concerning reproduction
outside the scope of the above should be sent to the Rights Department,
Oxford University Press, at the address above

You must not circulate this book in any other form
and you must impose this same condition on any acquirer

Published in the United States of America by Oxford University Press
198 Madison Avenue, New York, NY 10016, United States of America

British Library Cataloguing in Publication Data
Data available

Library of Congress Cataloging in Publication Data
Data available

Original Series, 26

ISBN 978-1-84-384101-2

CONTENTS

	PAGE
PREFACE	v
I. DAN JOHN GATTRYNGE'S SERMON	1
II. THE MIRROR OF ST. EDMUND	16
III. THE ABBEY OF THE HOLY GHOST	51
IV. WM. OF NASSINGTON'S POEM ON THE TRINITY, &C.	63
V. THANKS TO CHRIST	75
VI. A PRAYER TO CHRIST	77
VII. A PRAYER FOR MERCY	78
VIII. FIRST HYMN TO JESUS CHRIST	79
IX. HYMN TO JESUS CHRIST AND THE VIRGIN	83
X. A PRAYER TO CHRIST	87
XI. MORAL POEM	88
XII. A PRAYER TO JESUS	91
XIII. A SECOND HYMN TO JESUS	92
XIV. OF SAYNTE IOHN þE EUANGELIST	97
XV. EARTH UPON EARTH	106
XVI. SERVE AND LOVE CHRIST	107
XVII. WHAT THUNDER SIGNIFIES	114
XVIII. LAMENTATION OF A DYING SINNER	115
XIX. CHARM FOR THE TOOTHACHE	119
GLOSSARY	121
INDEX OF NAMES	131

PREFACE.

The miscellany of Religious Tracts and Poems which follows is edited from the Thornton Manuscript, which has already contributed the Morte Arthure and the Hampole Short Treatises to the publications of the E. E. T. S. It is hoped that it will serve somewhat towards illustrating the religious teaching of the fourteenth and fifteenth centuries, as well as towards exhibiting the peculiarities of the Northern English, in which all the pieces are written.

The first tract is a good and idiomatic specimen of a mediaeval Sermon, and as we find that it was preached in obedience to the command of 'oure Fadire þe byschope,' who had directed all those who under him had cure of souls 'opynly, one ynglysche, apone Sonondayes, to preche and teche þaym þat þay have cure off, the lawe and the care to knawe God Almyghty,' it is also at the same time an evidence of the amount of instruction provided for the people in those days. Some hundred years before this Sermon was written, Bishop Grosseteste had given very similar directions to his clergy, mentioning the very heads which are touched in this Sermon, and bidding them discourse of them to the people every Sunday *in idiomate communi*. Surely these facts, and many others like them which might be produced, go far to prove that the parish priest of the Middle Ages was not such a 'dumb dog' as some would have him to be, and that preaching was not confined to the Friars. Dan Jon Gaytrigg must have been a very sensible instructor for his flock, according to their creed and lights; and the nervous and rhythmical English in which his teaching is conveyed would be hard to equal in modern days. There is another copy of this Sermon in the Library of Trinity College, Cambridge, MSS. B. 10. 12, from which Prof. Skeat kindly made an extract for me. It differs very slightly from the text here printed, but has indications of being a somewhat later transcript. For instance, the old and probably not well-known word '*tray*' of the Thornton MS. is changed in the Cambridge copy into 'thoȝt', and an occasional omission of a Northern form betrays the fact that the copier was not writing his own dialect. Mr. Skeat, whose opinion on this subject is of the utmost weight, writes as follows with regard to the style of the Sermon. 'I have not a doubt that the "Sermon" was originally in *verse*, and to print it as prose, without remark, would be a mistake. It is to be noted that the Trinity MS. is at first written as prose (but there are frequent dots shewing where the lines end), and very soon it is written *as verse*, and so continues down to the end. For instance, look at the following:—

>Þe séxte poynt is . þát we sall tròwe
>þat þe foúrtyde dáy . áfter þat he ráse,
>thurgh stréngh of hemsélfe . he stéghed vntil héuen,
>whare oure kýnde is nów . in his blýssed pérson,
>noght ánely éuen . no méte til his aúngels,
>bot héghe corounde kýnge . abouén all aúngels.

It is clear that we have here the regular alliterative verse, *perfect* as regards accent, *imperfect* as regards alliteration; in fact, the very kind of metre into which the old Piers Plowman metre would naturally degenerate. The third line preserves the alliteration altogether, and is a nearly perfect line.' Perhaps even a stronger passage than the one selected by Prof. Skeat might be found at page 11:—

Eúynly to súffire . þe wéle and þe wáa,
Wélthe or wándreth . whéthire so betýde ...
Stýffely to stánde . agáynes our fáas,
Whéthir þay be bódyly . or þéy be gástely,
Swa þat ná fulle fándyng . máke vs to fálle,
Ne be fálse in our fáythe . agaýnes God Almýghtty.

Here the alliteration is very marked. I confess, however, I do not see my way to bringing the whole of the Sermon into this form. If it were originally written in alliterative verse, it would evidently have been with the object of helping the people to commit it to memory.

Treatise No. II is an old English translation of the Speculum of S. Edmund. This was a very popular treatise in its day, and, we believe, the only surviving work of the famous Edmund Rich, Archbishop of Canterbury—famous for his asceticism—famous as a teacher of Greek at Oxford, and as having had for his pupils Grosseteste, Robert, and Roger Bacon—famous for his sudden elevation to the Primacy—notably famous for the good stand he made in that office for English liberties—famous also for his retirement from his high post; and famous after death for the popular tumult which forced the pope to canonize him. All these points are well brought out in Dr. Hook's Life of the Archbishop. At the Monastery of Pontigny in France, the place of his retirement, where the great spirits of Thomas à Becket and Stephen Langton had before him found rest, he wrote, or at any rate finished, his *Speculum*. It is a composition which breathes a fierce asceticism, and is almost Manichean in its hatred of bodily ease. This would insure its popularity in an age which only comprehended religion as a bitter and unsparing chastiser of the flesh, and hence its early translation into French and English. We subjoin a specimen of the original, with the French and English translations. With regard to the age of the latter, Mr. Morris, on examining a passage sent to him, was of opinion that it might be as early as 1350. Very probably it is a rescript from a still earlier English version in a Southern dialect, but I have not discovered any other English MS. of this Treatise.

FRENCH.	LATIN. (*Original.*)	ENGLISH.
From Arundel MS. 288. p. 207.	From Magna Bibl. Vet. Patr. XIII. 355.	Thornton MS. (as printed).
Uidete uocationem uestram.—Ces moȝ de la postle partenent a nous genȝ de religion. ueeȝ, fet il, a quey uous estes apelleȝ. e ceo dit il por ceo quel homme¹ ke ieo pens de moy, mesmes de nuit e de iour, de une part ay ioye grant. e dautre part grant dolur. Ioye por la seynte religion. dolur en confusion por ma feble conuersacion. e ceo nest pas graunt merueyle. Kar Ieo ay grant acheson. Kar ci dit Seynt Eusebye en un sermon. uenir a religion est souereyne perfeccion. e nent parfitement uiure souerayne dampnacion. ¹ ? houre.	' Videte vocationem vestram fratres.' Ista verba apostoli pertinent ad homines religiosos. Videte (inquit) ad quid vocati estis. Et hoc dixit Apostolus ad excitandum nos ad perfectionem. Et propter hoc quâcunque horâ cogito de me ipso, die vel nocte, ex unâ parte habeo magnum gaudium, et ex aliâ parte magnum dolorem. Gaudium habeo propter sanctam religionem, dolorem et confusionem propter meam debilem conuersationem. Et illud non est mirum, quia habeo magnam causam. Nam, sicut dicit Sanctus Eusebius in vno ser-. mone, Venire ad Religionem summa perfectio est, sed non perfectè viuere in religione, summa damnatio est.	' Videte vocacionem vestram.' This wordes sayse Saynte Paule in his pystyll, and thay are thus mekill to saye one ynglysche, ' Seeȝe ȝoure callynge.' This worde falles till vs folke of religioune: and that sais He till excite vs till perfeccyone. And ther-fore what houre þat I thynke of my-selfe, one nyghte or on day, on a syde hafe I gret joye, and on anoþer syde gret sorowe —joy for þe haly religione, sorowe and confusyon for my febill conuersasione. And þat es na wondire for I hafe gret enchesone. Als þe wysse man salse in his sermon, he sais to com to religione es souerayne perfeccyone, and there - in noghte perfitly to lyffe es souerayne dampnacyone.

Among the promises of future publications made by the E.E.T.S. there is held out to us the hope of some day seeing in print the Life of S. Edmund from the British Museum MS. When it is printed I feel persuaded that it will be found very illustrative of the Speculum, and vice versâ. I believe Dr. Hook does not profess to have consulted this old mediaeval Life of the Archbishop for his biography in the third volume of his Archbishops.

We now come to No. III. The Abbaye of S. Spirit. This trea-

Preface.

tise, of which there are several MS. copies, has been attributed to various authors. Some would have it the composition of Bishop Alcock, who died 1480, but as it exists in the Vernon MS., which is about a century earlier, this notion is disposed of. In the Lambeth MS. it is given to Richard Rolle de Hampole, but as his paternity is claimed for almost all religious Middle-Age MSS. that have gone astray, we cannot build much on that. The fact of the early Vernon MS. having the Treatise in a Southern dialect is much against the supposition of its being Hampole's. Whether Robert Thornton re-wrote it in his own idiom, or how it got into the form we have here, cannot be discovered; but as the preference here given to the Thornton copy may seem to some to be unfounded, we subjoin a conspectus of a portion of four manuscripts for the purpose of comparison.

I. VERNON MS. (Bodleian.) A. D. 1380.	II. LAMBETH MS. 432. fol. 37 B.	III. TRIN. COLL. CAMB. MS. O. 1. 29.	IV. THORNTON MS. (as printed).
Here biginneþ a tretis þat is clept þe Abbey of þe holy gost. þat is conscience of monnes herte schulde ben in þis Abbey most.	Here begynnythe Rechard Hamppulle of the Abbay of the holy goest fulle nessessarye.	Þis es þe begynnynge of þe abbay of þe holye goste, þe wilke þates founded in A place þat es callede conscience, *and* perfore, mañ, be-whare!	Of the abbaye of saynte Spirite that es in a place that es callede conscyence.
Mi deore Breþren And Sustren. I seo wel . þat monie wolde ben In Religion . but þei mowe not . for Pouert. or for Age . or for drede of þeore kun. or for bond of mariage. And þerfore I make her a Book of Religion of herte . þat is of þe Abbeye	Dere Bretheryne and Sus*t*ren, I Se welle ther wold be many in Religeoun, but þay may not, for pouerte, or for Awe, or for drede of kyn, or for bondage, or for mariage; therfor y make here a boke of Religeoun of the hert That is of the Abbey of the holy	My fulle dere and well loued brethire and sisters i*n* god, I see now weel in þies dayes þat many meñ wilde full gladely be in religiou*n*, bot þei may nouȝt, fore pouerte or fore elde, or fore dreed, or elleȝ fore kyndrede or for bonde of mariage. And þerfore I make	A dere brethir and systirs, I see þat many walde be in religyone bot þay may noghte, owthir for pou*e*rte, or for drede of thaire kyn*e*, or for band of maryage, and for-thi I make here a buke of þe religeon of þe herte, þat es of þe abbaye of the Holy

of þe holi gost. þat alle þo þat mouwe not ben In bodi Religion þei mowe ben In gostly. Aʒ Jhesu Merci. Where may þis Abbey and þis Religion best ben I. founded. Certes neuere so wel. ne so semely. as in a place. þat is clept Concience. Now be houeþ hit þenne. at þe biginnynge. þat þe place of þe Concience be clanset. þorw wyʒ clansynge. þe holi gost senden a doun twey Maidens ful connynge. þat on is clept. Rihtwisnesse. And þat oþer loue of clannesse. þeose tweyne schul caste from þe concience and from þe herte all manere fulyth of foule þouʒtes and of foule ʒeornynges.

goest, that all tho that may not be in Bodely Religeoun myght be in goestly religeoun. A Ihesu mercy where may the abbay of this religeoun be best y foundid. Certis nowhwhere so wele ne so surely as in a place that is callid Consciens. Now hit behovith, at the bygynnyng that the place of the Conscience be clensyd wislye. The holy goest shalle Fynde two maydennys Fulle cunnyng, the tone is callid Rightwisnesse, And the tother is callid love of clennesse. These two shalle cast out from the conscience, and from the hert, alle maner Filthe of foule thoughtes and foule Desyris.

here now a boke of religione of þe herte, þat es, of þe abbaye of þe holy goste; þat all þoo þat may nouʒt be in bodily religione, þat þei maye godely be in gostely religioun. ¶ A Ihesu, mersy! where maye þis abbay and þis religione beste be foundeñ and groundede? ¶ Certeʒ, neuer nowere so well ne so stedefastlye, nor ʒit þerto so semely, as right in a placeʒ [1] þat þei calle conscience. ¶ Now þan behoues it firste at þe begynnynge, þat þe place of þe conscience be so enclosede on ilke syde thorough wies closynge, for þis encheson: ¶ Þe holy goste salle do sende two maydens full conande. ¶ þe tone is callede by clerkes Ryghtwysnes ¶ And þe tother is called lufe of grete (?) clennes. ¶ þies two maydenes sall keste fro þe conscience and fro þe herte all manere of fylthes and foule þoughtes, and of foule ʒernynges.

[1] sic in MS.; read "place."

Goste, that all tho þat ne may noghte be bodyly in religyone, þat þey may be gostely. A Ihesu mercy! Whare may þis abbaye beste be funded and þis religione? Now certis nowhare so well als in a place þat es called conscyence; and who so will be besy to funde þis holy religione, and þat may ilke gud crystyne mane and woman do þat will be besy þerabowte. And at þe begynnynge it es by-houely þat þe place of thi conscience be clensed clene of syne, to þe whilke clensynge the Holy Goste sall sende two maydyns þat ere comaunde, the one es callede Rightwysnes, and þe toþer es called Luffe of clennes. These two sall cast fro þe conscience and fro þe herte all maner of fylthe of foule thoghtes and desyrs.

It seems probable that II, III, and IV have been re-written from No. I in their different dialects, but at any rate this conspectus remarkably illustrates the well-known fact, that mediaeval copiers never kept close to their original, but altered and improved according to their own views of grammar and dialect, without any of that wholesome dread of omitting an inflection which is the scourge of modern editors. The Lambeth MS. in its latter part differs considerably from the Thornton, and contains several passages which the other has not. In fact it may almost better be described as a *similar* treatise than as identical. The Cambridge MS. shews a tendency to insert amplifications and additions, and would thus seem to be later in style, but Mr. Skeat says that the MS. looks like the fourteenth century. There are doubtless several other copies of the treatise to be found.

The matter of this treatise well illustrates the sort of notion which must always have existed even in the most palmy days of monasticism, viz. that it was just possible to live a religious life outside a convent. But the 'Abbaye of S. Spirit' further shews us the reluctance with which this was admitted, the attempt to clothe even active life with the forms, images, and duties of the cloister, and while admitting the possibility of its successful pursuit of holiness, at the same time putting by its side the far higher and more blessed state of the incarcerated regular.

The Religious Poem of William of Nassyngton is certainly not remarkable for its poetical genius, but in the simple scriptural statements of the quondam York lawyer we recognize with pleasure the mind of a devout layman rising out of distracting superstitions to a repose on the great eternal verities of the faith. The Hymns numbered VIII and IX both contain some simple and touching passages. The Moral Poem, No. XI, is by Richard Rolle de Hampole. Hymn No. XIII is among Dr. Furnivall's selections from the Lambeth MSS. There are differences here, but none, it is thought, will object to have two versions of such a beautiful and touching little poem. We now come to the most singular poem of the collection—Saint John the Evangelist. I have not hitherto heard of any other Manuscript of this, and I think all lovers of early English will not fail to be pleased with it.

Indeed some of the words were quite beyond my power, and must
have been left unattempted, but for the kind assistance given me in
this, and in many other points, by the Rev. W. W. Skeat.

I am afraid, taking the Miscellany throughout, rather a bitter
vein of religionism will be found to permeate it. Christianity
seems to be regarded as an institution for vexing and harassing the
human race, and everything connected with the body and its
belongings is simply evil. Manicheeism indeed, as Dean Milman
well points out, poisoned the very life-blood of mediaeval Christianity, and Augustine, while he overthrew it as a system, only
confirmed and established it as a sentiment. It is probable that
this sour asceticism, which has been remarkably illustrated by
several publications of the E. E. T. S., will come out even more
strongly, as the Society proceeds to dive deeper into the recesses of
old English. But this, at any rate, only makes us admire Chaucer
the more.

[The text of this book, as far as p. 18, was collated with the
Thornton Manuscript by Dr. Furnivall in 1906, and nine new
pieces, Nos. V, VI, VII, X, XII, XVI, XVII, XVIII, XIX, were
added to its contents. The Dean and Chapter of Lincoln kindly
consented to deposit the Manuscript in the British Museum, where
the Keeper of the Manuscripts, Mr. Gilson, was good enough to
receive it, and a fresh collation of the whole has now been made.
Since then the Rev. Canon C. W. Foster of Timberland has very
kindly looked up some readings in the MS., and a new Glossary
has been provided by Mr. O. T. Williams. J. M.]

I. DAN JON GAYTRYGE'S SERMON.

[*Thornton MS., Linc. Cath. Libr.*, leaf 213 back.]

Here begynnes a Sermon þat Dan Iohn Gaytryge made, þe whilke teeches how scrifte es to be made, & whare-of, and in scrifte how many thyngeȝ solde be consederide. Et est Petrus 4 sentenciar*um* discrecio*ne* primâ.

As a grett Doctour schewes in his buke, of all þe¹ creatoures þat Gode made in heuen and in erthe, in water and in ayere, or in oghte elles, þe Souerayne 8 cause & þe skyll whi He mad þam was His awen gud will and His gudnes, Thurgh þe whilke gudnes, alls He es all gude, He walde þat some creatures of þase þat He made ware communers of þat blyse þat euer-mare lastis. 12 And for þat na creatoure myghte come to þat blyse †withowtten knaweyng of Godd, als þat clerkes teches, He made skillwyse creatours Angelle and man, of witt and wysdom to knawe God Almyghtyn, and, thorowe þaire knawynge, lufe 16 Hym and serue Hym, and so come to þat blyse þat þay ware made to. This manere of knawynge had oure forme-fadyrs in þe state of Innocence þat þay ware mad In; and so sulde we hafe hade, if þay had noghte synnede. Noghte so mekill als 20 hally saules hase now in heuen, Bot mekill mare þan man hase now in erthe. For oure fourme-fadyrs synned, sayse þe prophete, and we bere þe wykkydnes of þaire mysdedis; For þe knawyng þat þay had of Godd All-myghten, they had it of 24 Goddes gyfte at þaire begynnynge, with-owtten trauayle, or tray, or passinge of tym. And all þe knaweyng þat we hafe in þis werlde of Hym, es of heryng, and of lerynge, and of techyng of oþer, of þe law and þe lare þat langes till Haly

God's mercy in Creation.

[†lf. 214.]
Man must have knowledge in order to obtain a share in it.

This must be gained by hearing and learning.

¹ MS. yᵉ. When y stands for þ, þ is printed. F.

I. Gaytryge's Sermon. The Six Things to be learnt by all.

Kyrke, þe whilke aƚƚ creatours þat lufes God Almyghteñ awe to knawe and to cuñ, and lede þaire lyfe aftiȝ, and swa come to þat blysse þat neuer mare blynnes.

And therefore those who have charge of souls must instruct them.

And for-thi þat mekiƚƚ folke now in þis werlde ne ere noghte 4 wele ynoghe lerede to knawe God Almyghty, ne lufe Hymͦ ne serue Hymͦ als þay sulde do, and als þaire dedys oftesythes opynly schewes, in gret pereƚƚ to þamͦ, to lyfe and to saule ; and perawnter þe defaute may be in thaymͦ þat hase þaiȝ saules 8 for to kepe, and thaymͦ sulde teche,—als prelates and persons, vicars and prestes, þat ere haldeñ by dett for to lere þamͦ—

Our father the Bishop has ordered all parish priests to instruct the people in their own tongue.

For-thi ouȝ Fadiȝ þe byschope þat God Almyghty saue, þat, als Sayñ Paule sayse in his pystiƚƚ, wiƚƚ þat aƚƚ meñ be safe, 12 and knawe God Almyghteñ, and namely þase vndirlowttes þat tiƚƚ hym langes, hase tretide and Ordeyned for þe comoñ profett, thorowe þe counceƚƚ of his clergy, þat ilkane þat vndiȝ hym hase cure of saule, Opyñly, one ynglysche, apoñ 16 sonnondayes, preche and teche þaymͦ þat þay hase cure off, þe lawe and þe lare to knawe God Almyghty, þat principally may

In these six things : (1) The fourteen points of the Creed, (2) the Ten Commandments, (3) the Seven Sacraments, (4) the Seven Works of Mercy, (5) the Seven Virtues, (6) the Seven Deadly Sins.

be schewede in theis sexe thynges—[1] In þe fourtene poyntes þat falles to þe trowthe, [2] In þe ten commandementes þat 20 Gode hase gyfeñ vs, [3] In þe Seueñ Sacramentes þat er in Haly Kyrke, [4] In þe Seueñ werkes of mercy vntiƚƚ oure eueñ crystyñ, [5] In þe seueñ vertus þat ilke mañ saƚƚ vse, [6] And in þe Seueñ dedly Synnes þat ilke mañ saƚƚ refuse. And he 24 byddes and commandes in aƚƚ þat he may, þat aƚƚ þat hase cure or kepynge vndiȝ hymͦ Enioyne þaiȝ parischennes and þaiȝ sugettes þat þay here and lere þise ilke sex thynges, and oftesythes reherse þamͦ tiƚƚ þat þay cuñ þamͦ, and sytheñ 28 teche þamͦ þaiȝ childiȝ, if þay any haue, whate tymͦ so þay

And Parsons and Vicars are to inquire at Lent whether their Parishioners know them.

are of elde to lere þamͦ. And þat persouns and vycars and aƚƚ parische prestis, Enquere delygently of þaiȝ sugettes In þe lentyñ tymͦ, wheñ þay come to scryfte, wheþer þay knawe 32 and cuñ þise sex thynges ; and if it be fundeñ þat þay cuñ þamͦ noghte, þat þay Enjoyne þamͦ appoñ his behalfe, and Of payne of penance, for to cuñ þamͦ. And for-thi þat nane saƚƚ excuse thaym thurghe vnknawlechynge for to cuñ þamͦ, 36

I. Gaytryge's Sermon. (1) The 14 Articles of the Creed.

ouꝛ haly Fadir † þe beschope, of his gudnes, hase ordaynede and bedyñ þat þay be schewede opynly one ynglysche amanges þe folke. [† lf. 214 back.] They are to be explained to folk in English.

4 Whare-fore, anence þe fyrste of þise sex thynges þat es to knawe, þe articles þat falles to þe trouthe,—als gret clerkes teches and schewes in thaire bukes,—Thare Falles to þe faythe¹ fourtene poyntes; Of þe whilke seueñ Falles to Goddes Godd- 8 hede, and oþer seueñ Falles to Cristes manehede. ¶ The firste poynte þat we sall trowe of þe Godhede, Es to trow stedfastely In a trewe Godd, and þat na noþer es for to trowe In. ¶ The toþer es, þat þe heghe Fadir of heueñ es stedfaste and sothefaste 12 Godd Almyghtyñ. ¶ The thirde es, þat Ihesu Criste, Goddes Sone of heueñ, es sothefastly Gode, eueñ till His Fadiꝛ. ¶ The ferthe es, þat þe Haly Gaste, þat samenly commes of bathe þe Fadir and þe Sonne, es sothefaste Godde, eueñ to þaym bathe; 16 and þe whethir noghte twa Goddes, þe Fadiꝛ and þe Sonne, ne thre Goddes, þe Fadir and þe Sonne & þe Haly Gaste, Bot thre sere persouns, and noghte bot a Godd. ¶ The fyfte arctecle es, þat þe Trynyte, þe Fadir and þe Sonne and þe Haly Gaste, 20 thre persouns and a Godd, es makere of heueñ and erthe and of all thynges. ¶ The Sexte artycle es, þat Haly Kirke, oure modire, es hallyly ane thorow-owte þe werlde, that es, comonynge and felawrede of all cristeñ folke þat comouns to-gediꝛ in þe 24 sacramentes, and in oþer haly thynges þat falles till Haly Kyrke, with-owtteñ þe whilke ne es na saule hele. ¶ The Seuend article þat vs awe to trowe es, vppe-rysynge of flesche, and life with-owtteñ Ende. For when þe dede hase sundyrde oure 28 bodyes and oure saules for a certayne tym, als oure kynd askes, vnto wheñ þat God sall deme þe qwykke and þe dede, Thane oure saules sall turne agayne till oure bodyes, and we þase ilke (and nane oþer þañ we are nowe), sothefastely sall ryse vp in 32 body and saule, þat neuer mare sall sundire, fra þat tyme furthe, bot Samen (if we wele doo whiles we er here) wende with Godd to þat blysse þat euer-mare lastes. And if we euyll do, till Endles payne.

And first of the fourteen Articles of the Creed.

Seven are of the Godhead.
(1) One true God.

(2) Father Almighty.

(3) God the Son.
(4) God the Holy Ghost.

(5) Three Persons and one God, Maker of all things.

(6) The Catholic Church, the Communion of Saints.

(7) The Resurrection of the Body and Life Everlasting.

¹ 'faythe' crost thru in the MS.

I. *Gaytryge's Sermon.* (1) *The 14 Articles of the Creed.*

Seven points of Christ's manhood.

¶ Thir are oþer seuen poyntes of Cristes Manhede þat are nedfull to trowe, till all þat are crystyn. ¶ The fyrste es, þat

(1) Incarnate of the Virgin Mary.

Ihesu Criste, Goddes Sone of heuen, was sothefastely conceyuede of þe maden Marie, and tuke flesche and blude, and become 4 man thurghe þe myghte and þe strenghe of þe Haly Gaste, with-owtten any merryng of hir modirhede, with-owtten any mynynge

(2) Both God and man.

of hir maydenhede. ¶ The toþer artecle es, þat we sall trowe þat He, Godd' and man bathe in a persoune, was sothefastely of 8 þat blessyde mayden, Godd' getyn of His Fadire be-fore any tyme, and man, born of His modir, and broghte furthe in tyme.

(3) Suffered for man.

¶ The thirde poynte þat we sall trowe es, Cristes Passione that He tholede bodyly for synfull man-kynde, How He was 12 betraysede with His disciple, and taken with þe Iewes, beten with scourges, þat na skynn helde, naylede one þe rude, and corounde with thornes, and many oþer harde paynes, and dyede

(4) Descended into Hell.

at þe laste. ¶ The ferthe artecle es, þat whene He was dede, 16 and His body tane doun, and wonden and doluen, ȝit þe whills His body lay in þe graue, þe gaste with þe Godhede wente vnto Helle, and heryede it, and tuke owte þase þat ware þare-in, als

[† If. 215.]

Adam and Eue and oþer †Forme-fadyrs whilke He in His forluke 20

(5) Rose again the third day.

walde þat ware sauede. ¶ The fyfte poynte es, þat one þe thirde day after þat He dyede, He rase fra dede to lyfe, Sothefaste Godd' and man in body and in saule. For als He dyede in seknes of oure manhede, So He rase thurghe strenghe 24 of His Godhede, and swa dystroyed oure dede thurgh His diynge, and quykkynd vs unto lyfe thurghe His rysesynge.

(6) Ascended into Heaven.

¶ The sexte artecle es, þat we sall trowe þat one þe fourtede day eftyr þat He rase, Thurgh strenghe of Hym-selfe, He steye 28 iu-till Heuen, whare oure kynde es nowe in His blyssyde persoune, noghte anely euynne ne mete till His angells, Bot hey corounde kynge abowne all His angells, þat be-fore tym was

(7) From thence He shall come to judge the quick and the dead.

lesse þan þe kynde of angells. ¶ The seuend article es, þat 32 righte als He dyede, and eftirwarde rase, and stey in-till heuen, Righte swa sall He come apon þe laste day, Bathe for to deme þe qwykke and þe dede, whare all þe folke þat euer was, or es, or sall be, sall sothefastely be schewede and 36

I. Gaytryge's Sermon. (2) The Ten Commandments.

sene be-fore Hym, and ilke a man answere of his awen dedis, and be saued or dampnede wheþer so he serues; For, als His ryghtwysenes now es mengede with mercy, swa sall it thane be
4 with-owtten mercy.

Secundo.
Decem precepta Dei.
The ten Commandementis.

8 ÞE secund thyng of þe Sex to knawe God Almyghten es, þe ten Commandmentes þat He hase gyffen vs. Of þe whilke ten, þe thre þat ere firste, awe us hallyly to halde anence oure Godd; and þe Seuen þat ere eftyre, anence
12 oure euen cristen. ¶ The firste comandement charges vs, and teches vs, þat we leue ne lowte na false goddes. And in þis commandement es forboden vs alkyn mysbyleues and · all mawmetryes, all false enchauntementes, and all soceryes, all
16 false charmes, and all wichecraftes, þat men of myssebyleue traystes appon, or hopes any helpe In, with-owtten God Almyghten. ¶ The toþer commandement byddes vs noghte take in ydillchipe, ne in vayne, þe name of oure Lorde Godd,
20 so þat we trowe noghte in His name bot þat es sothefaste, þat we swere noghte by His name bot it be byhouely, and þat we neuen noghte His name bot wirchipfully. ¶ The thirde commandement es, þat we halde and halowe oure haly day,
24 þe Sonondaye, and all oþer þat falles to þe ʒere, þat er ordeynede to halowe thurgh Haly Kyrke. In þe whilke dayes all folke, bathe lerede and lawede, awe to gyffe þam gudly to Goddes seruyce, to here and say it efter þaire state es, in wirchipe of
28 Godd All-myghty and of His gud halowes, noghte þan for to tente to tary with þe werlde, ne lyffe in lykynge ne luste, þat þe flesche ʒernes, Bot gudly to serue Godd in clennes of lyfe.
¶ The ferthe commandement byddes vs doo wyrchipe to Fadire
32 and to modire, noghte † anely to fleschely fadyr and modire, þat getes vs and fosters vs furthe in þe werlde, bot till oure gastely Fadire þat hase heuede of vs, and teches vs to lyffe till hele of

Secondly, of the Ten Commandments.

I. The first Commandment.

The second Commandment.

The third Commandment (4th of the Decalogue).

II. The fourth Commandment (5th of the Decalogue). [† lf. 215 bk.]

I. *Gaytryge's Sermon*. (2) *The Ten Commandments*.

oure saules, and tilł oure gastely modyr, þat es, Haly Kyrke, to be bouxome þare-to, and saue þe ryghte of it, For it es modir tilł alł þat cristenly lyffes, and alswa tilł ilke man þat wyrchipfulł es, for to do wyrchipe eftere þat it es. ¶ The fyfte 4 comandement byddes vs þat we sla na man, þat es to say, bodyly ne gastely noþer; For als many we sla, in þat at we may, als we sclaundire or bakbyte or falsely deffames, or fandes for to confounde þaym þat noghte serues, or withdrawes lyfelade 8 fra þam þat hase nede, if we be of hauynge for to helpe þam.

¶ The sexte commandment forbeddes us to syn or for to foly fleschely with any woman, owþer sybbe or fremmede, wedde or vnwedde, or any fleschely knawynge or dede haue with any, 12 oþer þan þe Sacrament of matremoyne excuseȝ, and þe lawe and þe lare of Haly Kyrke teches. ¶ The seuend' byddis vs þat we salł noghte stele: In whilke es forboden vs robbyng and reuyng, and alł wrangwyse takynge or with-haldynge, or 16 hydynge or helelynge of oþer menes gudes, agaynes þaire witt and þaire wilł þat hase ryghte to þaym. ¶ The aughten commandement byddes vs þat we salł bere no false wytnes agaynes oure euen cristen: In þe whilke es forboden vs alł 20 manere of lesynges, False consperacye and false swerynge, whare-thurghe oure euen cristyn may lese þayre catelł, Faith, Fauour or Fame, or anything elłs, wheþer it be in gastely or in bodyly gudes. ¶ The nyende commandement es, þat we ȝerne 24 noghte oure neghtboure house: In whilke es forboden alł wrangwyse couetyse of land or of lythe, or of oghte elles þat may noghte be lyftede ne raysede fra þe grounde, als thynge þat es stedfaste, and may noghte be styrrede. ¶ The tend' 28 commandement an þe laste es, þat we ȝerne noghte þe wyefe of oure neghteboure ne of oure euyn cristen, ne his mayden, ne his knaue, ne his oxe, ne his asse: In þe whilke es forboden vs to ȝerne or to take any thynge þat may be styrride of oþer 32 mēns gudes, als robes or reches or oþer catelł, þat we hafe na gude titilł ne na ryghte to; For what thyng so we take or getes one oþer wyse þan þe lawe and þe lare of Haly Kyrke teches, we may noghte be assoylede of þe trespase bot if we 36

I. *Gaytryge's Sermon.* (3) *The Seven Sacraments.*

make assethe, in þat þat we may, to þam̄ þat we harmede with haldande þaire gude. And in case þat we hafe thurghe false athes, als in assises or oþer enquestes, wetandly or willfully gerte oure eueñ cristyñ lesse þaire patremoyne or þaire heritage, or falsely be dyssessede of lande or of lythe, or false deuorce be made, or any mañ dam̄pnede, þofe all we do þat we may to þe party, ȝit may we noghte be assoylede of þe trespas, bot of oure beschoppe, or of hym þat hase his powere, For swylke caas es ryuely reseruede till hym̄ seluen̄. ¶ Thise ten commandementeȝ þat I hafe now rekkenede er vmbylowkede in twa of þe gospelle. The tane es, þat we luffe Godd' ouer all thynges; The toþer ✝ es, þat we lufe oure eueñ cristen̄ hallely in oure herte als we do oure seluen̄; For Godd awe vs to lufe hally with herte, with all oure myghte, with all oure thoghte, with worde and with dede. Oure euyñ crysten̄, als-swa awe vs to lufe vn-to þat ilke gude þat we lufe oure-selfe, þat es, þat þay wele fare in body and in saule, and come to þat ilke blysse þat we thynke to; and whate-so-euer þat he bee, þat þise twa wele ȝemes, all þe ten commandementes forsothe he fulfilles.

These Ten Commandments are included in two of the Gospels—that we love God and our brethren. [† lf. 216.]

Tertio.

Septem sunt Sacramenta Ecclesie.
The Seuene Sacramentes of Haly Kyrke.

PE thirde thynge of þe Sex þat I firste touchide, es þe Seueñ Sacramentes þat Haly Kirke gyffes, thurghe prelates and oþer prestes þat hase þe powere. Of whilke seueñ, the first fyve ilke cristeñ mañ awe lawefully to take efter his elde es; and twa lyes in þaire will þat ressayues þaym̄. ¶ The firste sacrament of seueñ es oure 'baptym̄,' þat we take þe firste tym̄ þat we be-com̄ cristyñ. In whilke, bathe þe firste synñ þat we ere borne with, and alkyñ oþer synnes, ere wascheñ awaye, þat we ere fylede with are[1] we take it; and þe trouthe of Haly Kyrke es takeñ þare-iñ, withowtteñ whilke na synfull mans saule may be sauede. And till þis sacrament Falles foure thynges, if it sall ryghtely be tane als Haly Kirke teches. Ane es, ryghte sayeyng and carpyng

The third thing is the Seven Sacraments.

The first is Baptism.

[1 before]

Four things required to make Baptism valid.

of þe wordes þat hym awe for to say þat gyffes þis sacrament, þat ere þise:—'I Baptise þe in þe name of þe Fadir and þe Sonne and þe Haly Gaste.' Ane oþer es, þat it be done anely in watire, For na noþer licoure es lefulle þare-fore. Þe thirde es, þat he þat gyffes þis sacrament be in witt and in will for to gyffe it. And þe ferthe es, þat he þat takes it be, noþer of lerede nor of lewde, Baptisede be-fore; For if he preste be in were of hym þat sall take it, whethire he be baptisede or he be noghte, þan sall he say þe wordes one þis wyese, 'If þou be noghte baptisede, I baptise þe in þe name of þe Fadire and þe Sone and þe Haly Gaste.' ¶ The secunde sacrament es 'confermynge,' þat þe byschope gyffes to þam þat ere baptisede, þat gyffes thorowe his powere to þam þat takes it þe grace and þe gyfte of þe Haly Gaste, to make þaym mare stalleworthe þan þay ware be-fore, to stande agaynes þe fende and dedly syn; þat nane hase powere to do bot þe byschope allane, þat hase the state and þe stede of Cristes Appostilles. ¶ The thirde sacrament es callede 'penance,' þat es, sothefaste for-thynkynge þat we hafe of oure syn, with-owtten will or thoghte to turne agayne to it. And þis sacrament must haue thre thynges:—Ane es, sorowe in oure herte þat we hafe synnede. Anoþer es, opyn scrifte of mouthe, how we hafe synnede. The [third es, satisfaccion, þat we maun do for oure syn]¹.
¶ Þise thre, with gud will to forsake oure syn, clensez vs and wasches vs of alkyn syn. ¶ The ferthe es, 'þe Sacrament of þe Autyr,' Cristes awen body in lyknes of brede, als hale als He tuke it of þe blysside mayden, the whilke, ilke man and woman þat of elde es, awe for to rescheyue anes in þe ȝere, þat es at say, at þe pasch, als Haly Kyrke vses, when þay ere clensede of syn thurghe penance, O payne of doynge owte of Haly Kyrke, bot if þay forbere it by skillwyse cause, þat awe to be knawen to þam þat sall gyffe it; For he þat tase it worthily, tase his saluacyone; and wha-so takes it vnworthily,

---

[1] Lf. 216 b. A sentence is here wanting through error of the scribe. [For 'satisfaccion' see Wm. of Shoreham's Poems 39/1078, 'Sorwe, schryfte, and edbote.' F.]

tase his dampnacione. ¶ The fyfte sacrament es 'þe laste Enoyn- *The fifth Sacrament is Extreme Unction.*
tynge with oyle,' þat es halowede and handelyde of prestes ; þe
whilke sacrament awe anely to be gyffen to þam þat he wate
ere of skillwyse elde, and þat he sese sekyrly in perelle of
dede, in lyghtenes and alegeance of þaire sekenes, if Godde
will þat þay turne agayne to þe hele, and als in forgyffnes of
venial synnes, and in lessynge of payne if þay passe heþen.

¶ The Sexte sacrament of Haly Kyrke es 'ordire,' þat gyffes *The sixth Sacrament is Orders.*
powere to þam þat ryghtwysly tase it, For to serue in Haly
Kirke efter þaire state es, and to þam þat takes þe ordyre of
proste, for to synge messe, and for to mynystre þe Sacramentes
of Haly Kyrke, þat to þam fallys, Eftyr þe state þat þay hafe,
and þaire degre askes. ¶ The seuend' Sacrament es 'Matry- *The seventh Sacrament is Matrimony.*
moyne,' þat es, lawefull festynnynge be-twyx man and woman
at þaire bathere assente, for to lyffe samen with-owtten any
lowssynge, whills þaire lyfe lastes, in remedy of syn and getynge
of grace, if it be tane in gude Entente and cleanes of lyfe.

The Ferthe thyng of þe Sex.

These be þe Seuene werkes of Mercy Bodyly.

Þe ferthe thynge of þe Sex to knawe Godd' Almyghty, þat *The fourth thing is the Seven Works of Mercy.*
vs byhoues fullfill in all þat we maye, ere þe seuen
dedis of mercy vntill oure euen cristen, þat Godd'
sall reherse vs apon þe dredfull day of dome, and wiet
howe we haue done þam here in þis lyfe, als sayne Mathewe *The 7 bodily Works.*
makes mynde in his gospelle. ¶ Of whilke, þe firste es, to 1.
fede þaym þat er hunngry. ¶ The toþer es, to gyffe þaym 2.
drynke þat er thristy. ¶ The thyrde es, for to clethe þam þat 3.
er clatheles or nakede. ¶ The ferthe es, for to herber þam þat 4.
er houseles. ¶ The fyfte es, for to vesete þam þat lyes in 5.
sekenes. ¶ The Sexte es, for to helpe þam þat lyes or er in 6.
presoun. ¶ The Seuend' es, to bery dede men þat hase myster. 7.
¶ Þise ere the Seuen bodyly dedis of mercy þat ilke man awe
to doo þat es myghtty. ¶ Þar are of mercy alswa Seuen gastely *The 7 spiritual deeds of Mercy.*
dedis þat vs awe to doo till þam þat hase nede till vs. ¶ Ane 1.
es, to consaile and wysse þam þat are wyll. ¶ Anoþer es, to 2.

I. *Gaytryge's Sermon.* (5) *The Seven Virtues.*

3. (†lf. 217.) chasty þam þat wyrkkys ill. ¶ Þe thyrd †es, to solauce thaym
4. þat er sorowefull, and comforthe thaym. ¶ The ferthe es, to
5. pray for thaym þat ere synfull. ¶ Þe fyfte es, to be thole-mode
6. when men mysdose vs. ¶ Þe Sexte es, Gladly to forgyffe when 4
7. men haues greuede vs. ¶ The seuend, when men askes vs for
[¹ MS. here] to lere¹ thaym, if we cun mare þan þay, for to lere thaym.
¶ Þise vn-till oure neghtebours ere full nedfull, and to þam þat
duse thaym wondir medefull; For he sall Mercy þat Mercyfull 8
es; and man with-owtten Mercy, of Mercy sall mysse.

The 7 Bodily Works in 1 line.
vij. opera *misericordie* corporalia :,: vnde *versus* :—
Vestio, cibo, poto, redimo, tego, colligo, condo.

The 7 Spiritual Works in 2 lines.
vij. opera *misericordie* spiritualia :—   12
Consule, castiga, solare, remitte, fer, ora,
Instrue, si po*teris*, sic *Christo* carus haberis.

The Fifte thyng of þe Sex.

The seuen*e* gastely vertus.   16

The fifth thing is the Seven Virtues.
Group 1 of 3.
Group 2 of 4.

PE fyfte thynge of þe Sex to knawe God Almyghten, are
þe Seuen vertus þat Haly Writte teches. Of whilke
seuen, þe thre first þat are hede thewes, teches vs how
to hafe vs vn-to God Almyghtty; and þe foure teches 20
vs swa for to lyffe þat it be bathe lykande to Godd' and to man.

I.
(1) Faith.
¶ Þe firste vertu es 'trouthe,' wharethurghe we trow anely in
Godd' þat made all thynges, with all þe oþer vertus I touchede
be-fore. And þis es nedfull till all þat cristenly lyffes; For 24
trouthe es begynnynge of all gude dedis; For noþer es trouthe
worthe with-owtten gud werk, ne na werke with-owtten trouthe

(2) Hope.
may pay Godd' Almyghtty. ¶ Þe toþer gude thewe or vertue
es 'hope,' þat es, a sekyr habydynge of gastely gude, thurghe 28
Goddes gudnes and oure gude dedis, for to com to þat blysse
þat neuer mare blynnes, Noghte anely in trayste of Goddes
gudnes, ne allanly in trayste of oure gude dedis, Bot in trayste
of thaym bathe when þay are bathe Sammen; For noþer sall 32
we fall sa ferre in-till whanhope þat we ne sall traiste to hafe

I. *Gaytryge's Sermon.* (5) *The Seven Virtues.*

þat blysse if we wele do; Ne we saɫɫ noghte com̄ so ferre in-to
ouerhope for to trayste so mekiɫɫ in Goddes gudnes þat we saɫɫ
hope to haue þat blysse with-owtten̄ gude dedys. ¶ Þe thirde (3) Charity.
4 vertue or thewe es 'charyte,' þe whylke es a dere lufe þat vs
awe vn-tiɫɫ Godd' Almyghtty als for Hym selfe, and tiɫɫ oure
euencristen̄ for God Almyghttyn̄; For þe tane may noghte
be lufede with-owtten̄ þe toþer, als Sayn Iohn þe gospellere
8 sayse in his pystiɫɫ. 'Þat commandement,' he saise, 'hafe we
of Godd'† þat wha-sa-euer lufes Gode, lufes his euencristyn̄. [†leaf 217 back.]
For he þat lufes noghte his broþer wham̄ he may see, how sulde
he lufe God wham̄ he sese noghte ?' ¶ Þe ferthe vertue or II.
12 thewe es 'ryghtwysenes,' þat es, to ȝelde to aɫɫ men̄ þat we awe (4) Justice.
þam̄, For to do to ilke a man̄ þat vs awe to doo, for to wirchipe
tham̄ þat ere worthy, For to helpe þe pure þat er nedy, to do
no gyle ne wrange vn-to na man̄, Bot for to do þat skiɫɫ es
16 vntiɫɫ ilke mane. ¶ Þe fyfte vertue or thewe es 'sleghte or (5) Prudence.
sleghenes,' þat wysses vs to be-warre with wathes of þe werlde;
For it kennes vs to knawe þe gud and þe iɫɫ, and alswa to
sundire þe tane fra þe toþer, and for to leue þat es euyɫɫ, and
20 take to þe gude, and of twa gud thynges for to chese þe better.
¶ Þe Sexte vertue es 'strenghe or stalworthnes,' noghte anely (6) Fortitude.
of body, bot of herte and wiɫɫ, euynly to suffire þe wele and þe
waa, welthe or wandreth, whethire so betyde, and þat oure herte
24 be noghte to hye for na wele-fare, ne ouermekill vndire for nane
euyɫɫ fare, Bot styffely for to stande agaynes oure faas, whethir
þay be bodyly or þay be gastely, swa þat na fulle fandynge
make vs to falle ne be false in oure faythe agaynes God Al-
28 myghtty. ¶ Þe Seuend vertue and þe laste es, 'methe or methe- (7) Temperance.
fulnes,' þat kepes vs fra owterage and haldes vs in euenhede,
lettes fulle lykynge and luste of þe flesche, and ȝemes vs fra
ȝernynges of werldly gudes, and kepes in clennes of body and
32 of saule. For methe es mesure and mett of aɫɫ þat we do, if
we lyffe skillwysly als þe lawe teches.

I. Gaytryge's Sermon. (6) *The Seven Deadly Sins.*

The sexte thyng and þe laste.

The sixth thing is the seven Deadly Sins,

PE sexte thynge, and þe laste of þase I firste towchede es, þe Seuen heuede or dedly synnes þat ilke a man *and* woman awe for to knawe to flee and forhewe, For folkes may noghte flee þam bot þay knawe thaym. ¶ Pride ¶ and Enuye, ¶ Wreth ¶ and Glotonye, ¶ Couetyse

Called Head Sins because all others spring from them:

¶ and Slouthe, ¶ and Lecherye. And for-þi er þay callede Seuen heuede Synnes, for þat all oþer commes of thaym; and for-þi er þay callede dedely synnes, for þay gastely slaa ilke manes & womanes saule þat es haunkede in alle or in any of thaym. Whare-fore þe wyese man byddes in his buke 'als fra þe face of þe neddyre, fande to flee syn.' For als þe venym of þe neddire slaas manes body, Swa þe venym of syn slaas manes

(1) Pride.

saule. ¶ The firste of þise Seuen synnes es callede 'Pryde,' þat es, a lykande heghenees of a manes herte, Of offyce or of heghe state, or oþer noblaye þat he ouþer haues of kynde or of grace, or he hopes þat he haues mare þan anothire. And of þis wikkede

[†lf. 218.]

synn commes some sere spyces:—Boste and † auauntynge and vn-bouxsomnes, despite, and ypocrisy and vnhamlynes, and oþer

(2) Envy.

þat ofte ere sene amanges prowde men. ¶ The secunde dedely synn es hatten 'Enuy,' þat es, a sorowe and a syte of þe wele-fare, and a ioy of þe euyll fare, of oure euencristen: Of whilke synn, many spyces sprenges and spredes. Ane es, hateredyn to speke or here oghte be spoken, þat may sown vn-to gude to þaym þat þay hate. Ane-oþer, false juggynge or dome of þaire dedis, and ay turne vn-to euyll þat es done to gude. Þe thirde es 'bakbyttynge,' to saye be-hynde þam, þat we will noghte avowe ne saye be-fore þam; whare noghte anely he þat spekes þe euyll, bot he þat heres it be spoken, es for to blame; For, ware þare na herere, þare ware na bakbyttere.

(3) Anger.

¶ Þe thirde dedly synn or heuede syn es 'wrethe,' þat es, a wykkede stirrynge or bollenynge of herte, whare-fore a man wilnes for to wreke hym, or wykkydly to venge hym, appon his euyncristyn. And of þis wykkede syn commes stryvynge and

I. Gaytryge's Sermon. (6) The Seven Deadly Sins.

flytynge, with many false athes and many foule wordes, Sclaundere, for to for-do a man's gude fame, Feghtynge and Felony, and ofte manes-slaughtere, and many ma þat nowe es [na] nede for to be neuenede. ¶ Þe fferthe dedly synn men calles 'glotonye,' (4) Gluttony. þat es, ane vnskilwyse lykynge or lufe in taste or in takynge of mete or of drynke. And þise trespas men duse apponne sere In 5 ways. wyse :—Ane es, ouþer ouer arely or ouer late, or ouer oftesythe, 1. for to ete or drynke bot if nede gere it. Ane oþer es, for to lyffe 2. ouer delycately. Þe thirde es, for to ete or drynke ouer mekyll. 3. Þe ferthe es, ouer hastely to ete or to drynke. Þe fifte es, to 4, 5. compas & caste appon whate wyese we may gette dylicious metis or drynkes to fulfill þe lykynges and þe lustes of þe flesch oþer þan we may gudly lede oure lyffe with, Secundum¹ versum,

Prepropere, laute, nimis ardenter, studiosè.   Versus.

¶ Þe fyfte dedly syn es callede 'Couetyse,' þat es, a wrangwyse (5) Covetousness. wilnynge or ȝernynge to haue any maner of gude vs awe noghte. And þis es donne pryncypally appon twyn wyese. Ane es, In 2 ways. wrangwysely to get any thynge þat oure likynge or oure lufe 1. lyghtes apon, als be Sacrelege or by symony, falsehede or okyr, or oþer gelery, whilke þise worldely men er wounte for to vse þat castes þaire conaundenes swa vn-to couetyse þat þay ne rekke wheþer it be with ryghte or with wrange, bot þat þay may gette þat at þaire herte ȝernes. Anoþer es, wrangwisely 2. to halde þat at es getyn, þat es, when we will noghte do to Godd Almyghten ne till Haly Kyrke, ne till oure euenn-cristyn, þat vs awe for to do by dett and by lawe, bot anely haldes þat we hafe for ese of oure selfen, whare noghte anely he þat wrangwysly getes, bot he þat wrangwysely haldes, falles in þe synn. ¶ Þe sexte dedly synn es 'slewthe or slawenes,' (6) Sloth. þat es, a hertly angere or anoye till vs of any gastely gud þat we sall do. †And of þis wikkede synn comes sere spyces :— [† lf. 213 bk.] Ane es, latesommes or lyte to drawe apon lenghte or to lache (1) lateness.

---

¹ MS. 'Sonde,' the probable miscopying of some contraction. Mr. J. A. Herbert suggests 'Secundum,' as the Latin words (not a verse) which follow mean 'Very hastily, delicately, too eagerly, anxiously,' state 4 of the abovesaid 5 ways to be avoided in eating and drinking.

I. Gaytryge's Sermon. (6) The Seven Deadly Sins.

(2) dullness.

(3) idleness.

any gude dedis þat we saꝉꝉ do þat may turne vs tiꝉꝉ helpe or hele of oure saules. Anoþer es, a 'dullnes or heuenes of herte' þat lettes vs, for to lufe oure Lorde God Almyghteñ, or any lykynge to hafe in His seruyse. Þe thirde es, 'ydillchipe,' þat 4 ouer mekyꝉꝉ es hauntede, þat makes lathe to begynñ any gude dedis, and lyghtly dose vs to leue wheñ oghte es beguñ, and þare whare we ere kyndely borne for to swynke, als þe feule es kyndely brede for to flie, It haldes vs euermare in ese agayne 8 oure kynde, For Idillnes es Enemy to cristeñ mañ saule, stepmodire and stamerynge agaynes gude thewes, and witter-

(7) Lechery, in

(1) fornication,

wyssynge and waye tiꝉꝉ alkyñ vices. ¶ Þe Seuend' dedely syñ es hatteñ 'lychery,' þat es, a foule lykynge or luste of þe 12 flesche. And of þis foule syñ comes many sere spyces :—Ane es 'Fornycacyone,' a fleschely synn be-twyxe ane anlypy mañ and ane anlypy womañ: and for-thi þat it [es] agaynes þe lawe, & þe leue and þe lare þat Haly Kirke haldes, it is dedly 16

(2) adultery,

syñ to þaym þat it duse. Anoþer es 'Avowtry,' and þat es spousebreke, wheþer it be bodyly or it be gastely, þat greuosere

(3) incest.

and gretter es þan þe toþer. Þe thirde es 'Incest,' þat es, wheñ a mañ synnes fleschely with any of his sybb frendes, or any 20 oþer þat es of his affynyte gastely or bodyly, wheþer so it be. Oþer spyces many sprynges of þis syñ þat ouor mokill on knaweñ and kende in þis werlde with þaym þat ledes þaire lyfe als þaire flesche ȝernes. 24

¶ Þise are þe sex thynges þat I hafe spoken off, þat þe lawe of Haly Kirke lyes maste in; The whilke we er

These things must be known if we would gain the bliss of heaven.

haldeñ to knawe and to cuñ, if we saꝉꝉ knawe God Almyghty, and come tiꝉꝉ His blysse. ¶ And for to gyffe 28 ȝow better wyꝉꝉ for to cuñ thaym, Oure ffadir þe beschope grauntes of his grace Fourty dayes of pardouñ tiꝉꝉ aꝉꝉ þat cunnes thaym, and ratyfyes alswa þat oþer meñ gyffes, Swa mekiꝉꝉ coueites he þe hele of ȝour saules. For ȝife ȝe 32 conandely knawe þise Sex thynges, thurgh thaym saꝉꝉ ȝe cuñ knawe Godd' Almyghty, whaym, als Sayne Iohn sayse in his gospelle, cunnandely for to knawe swylke als He es, It es endles lyfe and lastande blysse. To þe whilke blysse He brynge vs, 36

oure Lorde Gode Almyghty! Ameɴ! Ameɴ! Ameɴ! Per
Dominum nostrum Iesum Christum, qui cum Deo patrê [1] et
Spiritu Sancto viuit et regnat omnipotens deus in secula
seculorum. Amen! Amen! Amen!

[1] MS. patri.

[The 'Hymn to Jesus Christ'—Ihesu, thi swetnes, wha moghte it se—
printed on pages 92-6 below, follows here in the MS., on leaf 219.]

II. THE MIRROR OF SAINT EDMUND.

[*Robert Thornton's MS., Lincoln Cathedral Library*, lf. 197.]

¶ Incipit Speculum Sancti Edmundi Cantuarensis Archipiscopi in Anglicis[1].

Here begynnys The Myrrour of Seynt Edmonde þe Ersebechope of Canterberye.

I[2].

The writer addresses himself to the folk of religion, and exhorts them to live perfectly.

*V*IDETE *vocacionem vestram.* This wordes, sayse Saynte Paule in his pistyll, and thay are thus mekill to saye one ynglysche, 'Seese ȝowre callynge.' This worde falles till vs folke of religioun: and þat sais he, till excite vs till perfeccyone. And ther-fore, what houre þat I thynke of my-selfe, one nyghte or on day, On a syde hafe I gret Ioye, and on anoþer syde gret sorowe:—Ioy, for þe haly religioun; sorowe and confusyon for my febill conuersasione. And þat es na wondire, for I hafe gret encheson. Als þe wyese man saise in his sermon, he sais, 'to com to Religion es souerayne perfeccyone; and there-in noghte perfitly to lyffe, es souerayne dampnacyone.' And thar-for þare es na turne of þe way bot ane, to come in congregacyone, þat es, to drawe to perfeccione als þou will þi saluacyone, to leue all þat es in this worlde and all þat þer-to langys, and sett thi myghte to lyffe perfitly. To lyffe perfitly, as Sayne Bernarde vs kennys, þat es, to lyffe honourabilly, mekely, & lufesomly. Honourabilly, als to God, þat þou sett thyn Entente to do Hys will, þat es [at] say in all thynges þat þou sall thynke in hert, or say with mouthe, or doo in dede, with any of þi fyve wittes; alls with seynge of eghe,

II.

Perfect living consists in living honourably, meekly, and lovingly.
'Honourably' *implies doing God's will in all things.*

---
[1] *Verbis* understood.
[2] The numbers I, II, &c., at the side are not in the MS., but are appended to mark the chapters of the original Latin work.

II. St. Edmund's Mirror. Need of Knowing Ourselves.

Herynge of Ere, Smellynge of neese, Suellynge of throtte, towchynge of hande, Gangand, or standande, Lygand, or sittande, thynke at þe begynnynge if þat it be Goddes will or noghte. And if it be Goddis will, do it at thy powere. And if it be noghte Hys will, do it noghte, for to suffre þe dede.

Bot now may þou aske mee 'what es Goddes wyll?' I say þe, His will es na noþer thynge bot þi halynes. Als þe Appostill in his pystill :— ¶ **Hec est Voluntas Dei, Sanctificacio vestra**: þat es to say, þat es Goddes will, þat ʒe be haly. Bot now may þou aske me : 'What mase man haly?' I say þe, twa thynges with-owtten ma, þat es, knaweynge and lufe. Knaweyng of sothefastnes, and Lufe of gudnes. Bot to þe knaweynge of Godde, þat es sothefastnes, ne may þou noghte com Bot be knaweynge of thi selfe; ne ʒit to þe luf of Godde may þou noghte com, bot thurghe þe luf of thynn evyn-crystyn. To þe knaweyng of þi selfe may þou com with besy vmbythynkynge; And to þe knaweynge of Godde thurghe pure contemplacionne. To þe knaweynge of þi selfe þou may com on þis manere : Thynke besely and ofte what þou erte, what þou was, and what þou sall be. Fyrste, als vn-to þi body : þou erte now vylere þan any mukke ; þou was getyn of sa vile matire and sa gret fylthe, þat it es schame for to nevynn, and abhomynacyon for to thynke ; þou sall be delyuerde to tades and to neddyrs for to ete. What þou has bene and what thow erte, now sall þou als to þi saule, thynke, For what þou † sall be þou may noghte wyete nowe. Vmbethynke þe nowe how þou has don gret synns and many, and how thou has lefte gret gudnes and many. Thynke how lange þou hase lyffede, and what thow has rescheyuede, and how þou has dyspende it. For ilke an houre þat þou has noghte thoghte one Godde, þou has it tynte. For þou sall ʒelde resonne of ilke-ane ydill thoghte, of ilke-ane ydill dede, of ilke-ane ydill worde. And righte as þou has noghte ane hare of thi heuede þat it ne sall be gloryfyede, if swa be þou be safede, Righte swa sall eschape nane houre þat it ne sall [be] accountede. A Ihesu, mercy ! If all þis worlde ware full of

What the will of God is, viz. that we should be holy.

III.

Holiness consists in knowing and loving.

To know God we must know ourselves.

Reflect then on thyself. Thou art made of vile corrupting matter.

[† leaf 197 bk. Thow rep.] *Thou hast done many sins.* [MS. Thou sall.]

Thou must give account of all.

II. St. Edmund's Mirror. Reasons for Loving Jesus.

smaƚƚe powdire, wha sulde be sa qwaynte þat he sulde or moghte Iugge ilke a thoghte, ilke a sawe, ilke a dede by þaᵯ selfe, and twyᵰ ilke ane fra oþer? Certis na thynge bot þe saule, þat es a thowsande sythes gretter þan aƚƚ þis worlde, if it ware 4 a thowsande sythes gretter þan it es. And it es so fuƚƚ of dyuerse thoghtes, lykynges and ȝernynges, wha moghte þan thus seke his herte þat he moght knawe aƚƚ þat es þare-in or thynke it? See nowe, my dere hertly frende, howe þou 8 has gret nede of knawynge of thi selfe. Sytheᵰ aftyrwarde take gude hede whate þou erte nowe, als vn-to þi saule; howe þow has littyƚƚ of gude in the, and littiƚƚ of witte and littiƚƚ of powere; For þou ȝernys ilke a daye þat at noghte avayles 12 the, and euer mare ouer lattly þat at may availe the. Dere frende, þou erte dessayfede sa ofte with vayne Ioye; nowe trauelde with drede, nowe erte þou lyftede one lofte with false trayste. See now on þe toþer syde :—Þou ert chaungeabiƚƚ : 16 þat at þou wiƚƚ doo to day, þou wiƚƚ noghte to morne. And ofte sythes þou erte anoyede eftire many thynges, and turment if þou hafe thaym noghte. And sythen when þou has þaᵯ at þi wiƚƚ, þan erte þou of thaa thynges annoyede. Thynke ȝitt 20 one þe toþer syde, how þou erte lyghte to fande, frele to agayne-stande, and rody to assente. Off aƚƚ þese wrechidnes now has þe delyuerde Ihesu þi spouse, and delyuers þe ylke day mare and mare. For wheᵰ þou was noghte, He mad þe in saule 24 aftire His aweᵰ lyknesse and His ymage, and þi body made of foule stynkande skyūm of þe erthe, whare-of es abhomy-nacyone to thynke, He mad þe in witte and in membirs sa nobiƚƚ and sa faire þat nane caᵰ deuyse. Thynke now besyly, ȝe þat 28 has fleschely frendis and kynredyᵰ, why ȝe luffe þaᵯ sa derely and sa tendirly. If þou say þat þou lufes þi fadire or þi modire for-thi þat þou ert of þaire blude and of flesche getyᵰ, Sa are þe wormes þat comes of þaᵯ day be day. On a-noþer syde 32 þou has noþer of þaᵯ body ne saule, Bot þou þan has of God thurghe thayᵯ. For whate sulde þou hafe bene if þou had duellyde swilke as þou was of thayᵯ, when þou genderide in fylthe and in syᵰ? One þe toþer syd, if þou lufe brethire or 36

It is hard to search out all that is in the heart of man.

Our short-comings and imperfections are manifold.

Jesus the only deliverer from weakness and wretchedness.

He ought to be loved more than earthly friends.

II. St. Edmund's Mirror. The Infinite Mercy of Jesus.

systers or oþer kynredyn, for-thi þat þay are of þe same flesche *Reasons why we should love Jesus.*
of fadir or of modire, and of þaire blude, by þe same skyll solde
þou lufe a pece of þaire flesche if it [ware] schorne a-waye; and
4 þat solde be errour gret with-owtten mesure. ȝyfe þou say
þat þou lufes þam for-thi þat þay hafe fleschely fegure in lyknes [†leaf 198.]
of man, and for-thy þat þay † haue saule ryghte als þou has, þan
es þi broþer fleschely na nerre þan anoþer; bot in als mekill als
8 þou and he hase bathe a fadire and a modire fleschely, The
begynnynge of þi flesche, þat es, a lyttill filth, stynkande and
full to see. Thare-fore þou sall lufe Hym of whaym all þi
fairenes commes. And þou sall lufe gastely ilk a man, and
12 flee fra now-forthwarde to lufe fleschly. *IV.*

And swa sall þou doo certaynly if þou conabilly thynke of
gudes þat He has done gudly for þe; and mare sall doo if þou
lufe Hym enterely; For, als I saide at þe begynnynge,—when
16 þou was noghte, He made þe of noghte; and when þou was *The infinite mercies of Jesus.*
tynte, He fande þe; and when þou was peryschede, He soghte
þe; and when þou was saulde with syn, þan He boghte þe;
and when þou was dampnede, þan He sauede þe. And when
20 þou was borne in syn, He baptyȝede þe; and sythen aftirwarde,
when þou synnede sa foully and sa ofte, þan He sufferde þe
so frely, and habade thynne amendemente sa lange, and sythen
rescheyuede þe sa swetly, and þe has sett in sa swete a falachipe.
24 And ilke a day when þou mysdose, þan He reprofes þe; and *He always forgives us when we repent.*
when þou repentis þe, þan He forgyffes the; and when þou
erris, þan He amendis þe; and when þou dredis þe, þan He
leris þe; and when þou hungers, þan He fedis þe; and when
28 þou erte calde, þan He warmes þe; and when þou has hete, þan
He kelis þe; and when þou slepis, þan He saues þe; and when
þou rysez vpe, þan He vphaldes þe; and euer-mare when þou
erte at male eese, þan He comforthes þe. Thyre gudnes, and
32 many oþer, hase done vnto þe thi swete spouse Ihesu Criste.
And þe swettnes of His herte sall þou thynke euer-mare, and
euer speke þare-of, and euer-mare lofe Hym, and euer thanke *The service that we owe to Him.*
Hym, and that bathe nyghte & day, if þou oghte kan of lufe.
36 And þare-for, when þou ryses of þi bedde at morne or at *V.*

II. St. Edmund's Mirror. Prayers we should offer to Jesus.

mydnyghte, thynke als tite how many thowsand meñ & womeñ ere perischede in body or in saule þat nyghte: Some in fyre, Some in oþer manere, als in water or one lande; Some robbide, woundide, Slayne, dede sodanly with-owttyñ sacramentis, and 4 fallyñ in-till dampnacione ay lastande. Thynk alswa how many thowsande þat nyghte are in perill of saule, þat es to say, in dedly syñ, als in glotony, lechery, Couetyse, in manes-slaynge, and in many oþer folyes. And of all þise illes, 8 the has delyuered thy swete Lorde Ihesu, with-owtteñ þi deserte. What seruyce hase þou donne, whare-fore He hase þusgate keped þe, and many oþer loste and forsakeñ? For sothe, if þou take gud kepe how gret gude He has done þe 12 on ilk a syde, þou sall fynd hym ocupiede aboute þi profet, als He did nañ oþer thynge, bot anely ware entendande to þe and to þi hele, als if He had forgetyñ all þis worlde for to be anely intendand' vn-to þe. ¶ And when þou hase þis 16 thoghte, lyfte vpe thi handis and thanke thi Lorde of þis and of all †oþer gudes, and say one þis manere, 'My[1] Lorde Ihesu Criste! grace I ȝelde; and thanke þe, þat me, thyne vnworthy seruande, þou hase kepid couerde and vesete in þis 20 nyghte (Or in þis day), hale, safe, and wemles vn-to þis tyṁ þou hase made to come, and for all oþer gudes and benefitis þat þou hase geffyñ me, anely thurghe þi gudnes and þi pete, þou þat lyffes and regnes endles. Ameñ.' Dere frende, in þis 24 same manere sall þou say when þou rysez at morne, and when þou lygges downñ at evyñ. And wheñ þou has done swa, þan sall þou besyly thynke how þou hase spende þat day (or þat nyghte), and pray God' of mercy of þe ill þat þou hase done, 28 and of þe gude þat þou hase lefte vn-till þat tyṁ. And, dere frende, do na thynge in þis lyfe till þou commend þi selfe, and thi frendes qwykke and dede, in the handis of thi swete Lorde Ihesu Criste, and say one þis maner, 'Lorde[2] Ihesu Criste! in 32

[†leaf 198 bk.]
The prayers we ought to offer to Christ.

Do nothing till you've commended yourself and your friends to God by prayer.

[1,2] These prayers are first given in the MS. in Latin—*Gracias tibi . . . In manus tuas . . .*—the translation immediately following. It did not seem necessary to print the Latin as well, the English being a full equivalent. The translation in the first case is introduced with the words 'This Orysoñ es þus to say one Inglysche my Lorde,' &c.; and in the second ' And þis orysone es þus mekill to saye Lorde ' &c.

II. St. Edmund's Mirror. Contemplation of God.

þi handis, and in þe handis of thyn̄ haly Angells, I gyffe in *The Prayer to Jesus Christ.*
þis nyghte (or in þis day) my saule and my body, my Fadir
and my Modire, my brothire and my systirs, frendis and
seruandes, neghtburs and kynredyn̄, my gude-doers, and all
folke righte trowande. Kepe vs, Lorde, in þis nyghte (or
þis day) thurgh þe gud dedis and þe prayere of þe blyssed
mayden̄ Marie and all thi halous, fra vices and fra wykked
ȝernyngez, fra synns and fra fandynges of þe deuell, fra sodayne
and avysede dede, and fra þe paynes of helle. Lyght my
herte of the Haly Gaste and of thi haly grace! Lorde! þou
make me to be bouxsome euer-mare to þi byddynges, and suffire
me neuer mare to twyn̄ fra the, endles Ihesu, Lorde in Trinite!
Amen!' My dere frende, if þou hase þis manere, þan sall þou *Thus we may obtain the*
hafe verray knaweynge of thi selfe, For thus saise haly Writte, *knowledge of ourselves.*
'If þou † trayste one thy selfe, to þi selfe þou sall be takyn̄; [†leaf 199.]
and ȝif þou trayste one Gode and noghte one þi-selfe, to God
þou sall be gyffen̄.' And þis maner of consederatyone es
callede 'medytacyone,' For by þis maner of knawynge of þi
selfe, & by þis maner of medytacyone, sall þou come to þe
knaweynge of Gode, by haly contemplacyone.

Wiet þou þat þare es thre manere of contemplacyone. The VI.
fyrste es in creaturs. The toþer es in haly scripture. The *The three different sorts*
thirde es in Gode hym-selfe in His nature. Thow sall wyet þat *of contemplation:*
contemplacyone es na noþer thynge bot thoghte of Godde
in gret lykynge in saule, And to se His gudnes in His creaturs.

His gudnes in His creaturs may þou see one þis manere. Thre *Contemplation of the*
thynges pryncypaly ere in Gode, þat es to say, Myghte, *works of God;*
Wysdome, and gudnes. Myghte es appropirde to Godd þe
Fadire. Wysdome, to God þe Son̄. Gudnes, to God þe Haly
Gaste. Thurgh Goddes myghte ere all thynges made, and
thurgh His wysdome ere all thynges meruailously ordaynede;
and thurgh His gudnes ilke a day ere all thynges waxande.
His powere may þou see by þaire gretnes and by thaire makynge;
His wysdom̄ by þaire fairenes of þaire ordaynynge; His gudnes
may þou see by þaire Encressynge. Þaire gretnes may þou see
by þaire four partynges, þat es to saye, by þaire heghte, and by

þaire depnes, and by þaire largenes, and by þaire lenghe. His wysdom may þou see if þou take kepe how He hase gyffen to ylke a creature to be. Some He hase gyffen to be anely, with-owtten mare, als vn-to stanes. Till oþer to be & to lyffe, als to grysse and trees. Till oþer to be, to lyffe, to fele, als to bestes. Till oþer to be, to lyffe, to fele, and with resone to deme, als to mane and to angells. For stanes erre, bot þay ne hafe nogte lyffe, ne felys noghte, ne demes noghte. Trees are; þay lyffe, Bot thay fele noghte. Men are; þay lyffe, þay fele, and þay deme, and þay erre with stanes, [þay] lyffe with trees, þay fele with bestes, and demys with angells. Here sall þou thynke besyly þe worthynes of manes kynde, how it ouer-passes ilke a creature. And þare-fore saise Saynt Austyn, 'I wald noghte hafe þe stede of ane angelle, if I myghte hafe þe stede þat es purvayede to man.' Thynk also þat man es worthy gret schenchipe þat will noghte lyffe eftyre hys degre and eftyre his condicyone askis; For all þe creaturs in þe worlde ere made anely for man. Þase þat ere meke, ere made for thre skylles; For to helpe vs at trauayle, als nate, Oxen, kye and horse; For to couer vs & clethe vs, als lyne, and wolle and lethire; for to fede vs and vphalde vs, als bestes, Corne of þe ertho, Fysche of þe See; and þe noyande creaturs, als ill trees and venemous bestes, þe wylke are made for thre thynges, For oure chastyyng, for oure amendement, and for oure kennynge. We ere chastied and puneschet, when we ere hurte. And þat es gret mercy of Godde, þat He will chasty vs bodyly þat we be noghte punescht lastandly. † We erre amendid when we thynke þat all þese ere broghte vs for oure syn. For when we see þat sa lyttill creaturs may noye vs, þan we thynke one oure wrechidnes, and þan we ere mekyde. We ere Eftir-warde kende, for-þi þat we see in þise creaturs þe wondirfull werkes of God oure Makere. For mare vs availes till oure ensampill and Edifycacione, þe werkes of þe pyssmowre þan dose þe strenghe of þe lyone or of þe bere. Als-swa, righte als I haue said of bestes, reght swa vndirstande of trees; and when þou hase donne on þis manere, Raise vp thy herte vn-till

II. St. Edmund's Mirror.   Contemplation of God.

Godd, and thynke how it es grete myghte to make aƚƚ thynges of noghte, and to gyffe þam to bee, and grete wysdom̅ to ordayne þam in sa gret fairenes, and in swa gret bounte, to multyply
4 þam̅ ilk a day for oure prowe. A! mercy Godd! how we are vnkynde! We dyspende aƚƚ His creaturs, and He þam makes! *The thoughts this should cause in us.* We confound þam̅, and He þam̅ gouernes. We distruy þam̅ ilke a day, and He þam multyplies. And þare-fore say tiƚƚ
8 Hym in thi herte, 'Lorde! for-þi þat þou arte, þay ere, and for-þi þat þou arte fayre, þay are faire; and for-þi þat þou arte gude, þay are gude. With gud ryghte þay loue þe, and Onoures þe, and gloryfyes þe, aƚƚ thy creatures. O blyssed Godd in
12 Trinyte! with gud ryghte þay loue þe for þaire gudnes, with gud ryghte þay anouren̅ þe for thaire fairenes, with gud righte þay glorifye þe for þaire profet, aƚƚ þi creaturs, blyssed Trinyte! Of wham̅ aƚƚ thynges ere thurgh His powere made; Thu[r]gh
16 whaym aƚƚ thynges are thurgh Hys wysdom̅ gouernede; In whaym aƚƚ thynges are thurgh His bounte multipliede; Tiƚƚ Hym honour and louynge with-owten̅ [ende]. Amen̅!'

20 ÞE toþer degre of contemplacyone es in Haly Wryte. *ij^a pars.* Bot nowe may þou say to me, 'I þat knawes na letters, **VII.** how may I euer mare com to contemplacyone of Haly *The second sort of contemplation is of Holy Writ.* Writte?' Now, my dere frende, vndirstande me swetely, and I saƚƚ say perchance to þe aƚƚ þat es wreten̅, if þou kan̅ noghte
24 vndirstand Haly Writt. Here gladly þe gud þat men̅ saise þe: *How the unlearned may profit by Holy Writ.* and when̅ þou heres Haly Wryte, owþer in sermon̅ or in priue collacyone, take kepe als tyte, if þou here oghte þat may availe þe tiƚƚ edyfycacyon̅, to hate syn̅ and to lufe vertue, and to
28 dowte payne, and to ȝerne Ioye, To dispyse þis worlde, and to hye to blysse, and whate þou saƚƚ doo and whate þou saƚƚ lefe, and aƚƚ þat lyghtes þinne vndirstandynge in knawynge of sothefastnes, and aƚƚ þat kyndiƚƚs þi lykynge in brynnynge
32 of charite; For of þise twa gudnes, es aƚƚ þat es wretyn̅ in preue or in apperte. Owte of haly writte sall þou drawe and cun̅ witte, whilke are þe seuen̅ dedly synnes, and þe seuen̅ vertus, and þe ten †comandmentis, and þe tuelfe artycles of [† *leaf 200.*]
36 þe trouthe, and þe seuen̅ sacramentis of Haly Kyrke and þe

seueñ gyftis of þe Haly Gaste, and þe seueñ werkes of mercy, and þe seueñ vertuz of þe GospeH, and þe seuen prayers of þe pater noster.

VIII.

The seven deadly sins.

Þir are þe seueñ dedly synnes :— 4

(1) Pride. Its seven disobeyings to God.

Pryde and Envy, Ire, Slouth, Couetyse, Glotony and Lechery. Pryde es lufe of vnkyndly heghyng; and þar-of comes þir seuen vnbouxomnes agayne God, or agayne souerayngne, þat es to say, to lefe þat þat es commandyd, and 8

(2) Surquedry.

to do þat that es defendyde. The toþer branch of pride es surquytry, þat es, to vndirtake thyng ouer his powere, or wenys to be mare wyse þan he es, or better þan he es, and auauntez hym of gude þat he hase of oþer, or of iH þat he hase 12

(3) Hypocrisy.

of hym-selfe. The thrid braunche of pride es ypocrisye, þat es, wheñ he feynys hym to hafe gudnes þat he hase noghte,

(4) Contempt.

and hydes þe wykkednes þat he hase. The ferth braunch of pride es despyte of thyne euencristeñ, þat es, when man lesses 16

(5) Excuses.

gudnes of oþer, for-thi þat hym selfe suld seme þe bettir. The fyfte braunche, þat es, when man makes lyknes be-twyx his aweñ wykkednes and oþer mens wikkednes, þat his aweñ may

(6) Shamelessness.

seme þe lesse. The sexte braunche of Pryde es vnschamefulnes, 20

(7) Elation.

þat es, when men hase noghte schame of iH ded aperte. The seuoñ braunche of pryde es Elacioñ, þat es, when a man hase heghe herte, þat he wiH no3te suffire to felawe ne mayster.

Man prides himself on three things.

Dere frende, þou saH wit þat thre thynges ere, whare-of a man 24 Enprides hym, þat es to say, of þe gudez þat he hase of kynde,

1. als fairenes or strenghe or of gude witte or of nobiHe kynredyñ.

2. The toþer thyng es þat men hase of purchase, als cunnynge,

3. Grace, gud loos, or dygnyte or offyce. The thirde thynge es 28 erthely thynge or erthely gude, als clethynge, houssynge, Rentez, Possessioñ, Men3e, horssyng, and honour of þis worlde. Pride makes man to be of gret herte and heghe, to despyse his euencristeñ, and to 3erne heghenes and maystry ouer oþer. 32

(2) Envy.

The toþer dedly syñ es 'Envy.' And þat es, Ioye of oþer mens harme, and sorowe of oþer mens wele-fare. And þat may be in herte with lykynge, or in mouth with bakbyttynge, or in werke with of mens gudnes wythdrawyng, or eHs with iH procurynge. 36

II. St. Edmund's Mirror. Remedy for Sin. Seven Virtues.

Envye mase man to hafe þe herte hevy of þat he sese oþer men mare worthi þan he in any thyng. The third dedly syn̄ es (3) Anger. 'wrethe,' þat es, ane vnresonabyll temperoure of herte; and of it
4 comes stryfes and contekes schamefull, and dyuerse wordes, and deuyouse and wikked sclandirs. † The ferthe dedly syn̄ es (4) Sloth. 'slouthe;' and þat mase manes herte hevy and slawe in gude [† leaf 200 bk.] dede, and makes man̄ to yrke in prayere or halynes, and puttes
8 man in wykkednes of wanhope, for it slokyns þe lykynge of gastely lufe. ¶ The fyfte dedly syn̄ es 'couetyse,' and þat es, ane (5) Covetousness. vn-mesurabill luffe to hafe erthely gudes; and it destroyes & blyndes manes herte. And þare-of commes tresones, False
12 athes, wykked reste, Malice, and hardnes of herte agaynes mercy. ¶ The sexte dedly syn̄ es 'glotony;' and þat makes man̄ (6) Gluttony. to serue and to be bouxome till wykked lykynges of þe flesche, þe whilke man suld maister and ouercome with mesure. Of
16 glotony commes vayne Ioy, lyghtnes, and littill vndirstandynge. ¶ The seuen̄ dedly syn̄ es 'lecherye;' and þat mase manes herte (7) Lechery. to melte, and to playe thare þare his herte lykes, and heldes, and þat with-owten̄ gouernynge of resoune. Of lechery
20 commes blyndynge of herte, in prayere vnstabilnes and fulle hastynes, lufe of hym selfe, hatreden̄ of Godde, lufe of þis worlde, vgglynes, and whanhope of þe blysse of heuen̄. ¶ Dere Why these are deadly frende, thire are þe seuen̄ dedly synnes; and wele ere þay callid sins.
24 dedly synnes, For Pride twynnes fra man his Godde, Envy his euencristen̄, Ire hym-selfe twynnes, Slouthe hym tourmentes, Couetyse hym be-gyles, Glotony hym dessayues, and Lecherye hym in thraledome settis.
28 Nowe hase þou herde þe seuen̄ sekenes of manes saule. IX. ¶ Sythen̄ aftirwarde commes þe souerayne leche, and takes þere medcynes, and waresche man̄ of þese seuen̄ seknes, and stabills hym in þe seuen̄ vertus3, thurgh þe gyftes of þe Haly Gaste.
32 Þe whilke are þese, ¶ þe gaste of wysdom and vndirstandynge, The seven Christian þe gaste of consaile and of stalworthenes, þe gaste of cunnynge Virtues. and of pete, and þe gaste of drede of Godde Almyghty. Thurghe þese gyftes oure Lord Ihesu lerres man̄ all þat he hase myster
36 till þe lyfe þat es callid actyfe, and til þe lyfe called contem-

platyfe. And se howe firste, maṅ suld lefe þe euyll and do þe
gude: lefe þe euyll, þat teches vs þe gaste of drede of Godd'
Almyghty; and do þe gude, [þat] leres vs þe gaste of pete.
And for-þi þat twa thynges are þat lettis vs to do gude, that
es at saye, wele-fare and tribulacione of þis worlde; For wele-fare
desayues vs with losengery, tribulacioṅ with hardnes of noyes
& dysses; for-þi sall þou despyse þe wele-fare of þis worlde, þat
þou be noghte þer-with dessayued; and þat leres þe þe gaste of
cunnynge; and þou sall stallworthly suffire tribulacyoṅ, þat
þou be noghte ouercommeṅ; and þat teches vs þe gaste of

Four of these needful for the active life. stallworthenes. And þire foure suffice till þe lyfe þat es callid
actyfe. And þe toþer thre fallys to þe lyfe þat es callid con-
[†leaf 201.] templatyfe, †For thre maners of contemplacioṅ. Ane es in
The other three for the contemplative life. creaturs; and þat leres þe gaste of vndirstandynge. The toþer
es in Haly Writte, whare þou sese whatte þou doo & what þou
sall lefe, and þat leres þe the gaste of consaile. The thirde
manere es in Godde Hym-selfe; and þat leres vs þe gaste of
wysdoṁ. Now þou sese thurgh þe gyftes of Ihesu, how He es
besy abowte oure hele.   Eftire þis sall þou wiete whilke ere

X. þe teṅ comandementis. ¶ Þe firste comandement es þis, 'Thow
The ten Commandments. sall wirchippe bot a Godde, þi Lorde, and till Hym anely þou
The first Commandment. sall seruo.' Þat es at say, wyrchipe Hym with righte trouthe,
Serue vntill anely with gude werkes. Here sall þou thynke
if þou hafe lelly serued Godde & wirchiped Godde; if þou hafe
seruede Hym ouer all thynge, if þou hafe ȝolden Hym þat that
þou hyghte, or if þou hafe done lesse penance, and if þou hafe
ȝoldyṅ Hym þat that þou hyghte Hym in þi cristyndoṁ, That
was, to forsake þe deuelle and all his werkes, and in God lelly
to trowe. And thurghe þis commandement es maṅ ordaynede
The second Commandment. ynence God þe Fadire. ¶ Þe toþer commandement es defendid to
take Goddes name in vayne; and lying and falsenes þare-in es
defendid'; and thurghe þis commandement es man ordaynede
ynence Godd' þe Soṅ, þat saise Hym-selfe 'I am sothefastnes.'
The third Commandment (4th of Decalogue). ¶ Þe thirde commandemente es, 'vmbythynke þe þat þou kepe
þe haly-dayes,' þat es to saye, in þine aweṅ herte, to kepe þe
in riste and pees with-owtteṅ seruage of syṅ or of bodyly

II. St. Edmund's Mirror. The Ten Commandments.

dedis. And þis commandement ordaynes man to reschayfe
þe Haly Gaste. Þise thre commandmentes lerres man how- *These three as to God.*
gates he sall hafe hym ynence Godd' þe Trynite, to whas lyknes
4 he es made in saule. Þe oþer seuen commandementes leres *The other seven as*
man how he sall hafe hym ynence his euencristen. ¶ Þe firste *to fellow-Christians.*
es, 'þou sall honour þi fadire and þi modire fleschely and *The fourth*
gastely, and þat in twa maners, þat es to say, þat þou be *Command-ment (5th of*
8 bouxom to thaym in reuerence and honour, and þou helpe þam *Decalogue).*
at thy powere in all thynges þat þay hafe myster, þat þou be
of lange lyfe in erthe; For if þou will be of lange lyfe, it es
reson þat þou honoure thaym of whaym þou hase þe lyfe; For
12 he þat will noghte honoure hym thurgh whaym he es, it es
noghte righte þat he be mare þan he es. ¶ Þe toþer commande- *The fifth*
ment es þis, 'Þou sall sla na man.' Here sall þou wyt þat *Command-ment (6th of Decalogue).*
slaughter es of many maneres. For þer es manes-slaghter of
16 hand, of tunge, of herte. Mannes-slaynge of hande es when
a man slaes anoþer with his handez, or when he duse hym in
bandis of dede, als in preson or in oþer stede þat may be
encheson of his dede. Manes-slaynge of tunge es in twa
20 maners, thurghe commandement, or thurghe enticement.
Manes-slayng of herte es alswa one twa maners, þat es, when
men ȝernys and couaytes ded of oþer, and when he suffyrs man [† lf. 201 bk.]
to dy, † and will noghte delyuer hym if he hafe powere. ¶ Þe *The sixth Command-*
24 thirde commandement es þis: 'Þou sall do na lechery;' and *ment (7th of Decalogue).*
þat es ryghte. Wha-sa will hafe þe lyfe with-owtten corupcyone
in þe Ioy of heuen, hym byhoues kepe his lyfe þat es dedly,
with-owtten corupcione of body. ¶ The ferthe commandement *The seventh Command-*
28 es þis, 'Þou sall do na thyfte ne na falsenes;' and þat es ryghte. *ment (8th of Decalogue).*
For he þat will safe oþer menes lyfe, he sall noghte do away þat
that moghte his lyfe sustayne. ¶ The fyfte commandement es *The eighth Command-*
þis, 'Þou sall noghte bere false wittnes agaynes thyne euen- *ment (9th of Decalogue).*
32 cristyn with hym þat will noye hym or sla hym.' And þat es
ryghte; For he þat will noghte sckathe his euencristyn, he
sall noghte consente, ne na consaile gyffe, to do hym ill. ¶ Þe *The ninth and tenth*
sexte commandement and þe seuend' er þir, 'Þou sall noghte *Command-ments (10th*
36 couaite þi neghtboure wyfe, ne þou sall noghte couaite his *of Decalogue).*

house, ne nane of his gude wrangwysly,' For he þat hase
wykked will and ill Entente in his herte, he may noghte lang
with-haldynge hym fra wykkide dede; and þer-fore, if þou will
noghte do lecherye, þou sall noghte consente to maṅ ne to
womaṅ þat it duse; and if þou will noghte stele, þou sall
noghte couayte oþer mennes thynges in þi herte. Dere frende,
þir are þe ten commandementes þat God gafe till Moyses in the
mounte of Synay. The thre fyrste er pertenande to þe lufe of
God, and the toþer seueṅ to þe lufe of þi-selfe and of thyne
eueṅ crystyṅ.

XI. Now, efter, sall þou wyt whilke ere þe seueṅ vertusȝ, þat es to
saye ¶ Trouthe, Trayste, and lufe, Wysedoṁ and Rightwysenes,
Mesure and Force. Of þe same matire er þe seueṅ vertus þat
þe teṅ commandementis, bot þis es þe varyance be-twyx thaym:
The teṅ commandmentis kennes vs what we sall do, and þe
seueṅ vertus kennes vs how we sall doo. The thre fyrste, þat
es to say, Trouthe, trayste and lufe, ordaynes the how þou
sall lyfe als to Godd': þe toþer foure how þou sall ordayne thyne
aweṅ lyfe þat sall lede till þe Ioye of heueṅ. Dere frende,
the awe to wyt þat we ere all made for ane End, þat es to say,
for to knawe Godde, to hafe Hym, and to lufe Hym. Bot thre
thynges or nedefull at puruaye till oure cunnynge, That es to
wyte, whedyr we sall ga, and þat we wyll comme thedyre, and
þat we hafe trayste to com thedyre; For grete foly ware it to
be-gyṅ þe thynge mane may noghte ende; ȝitte, one þe toþer
syde, þe mane þat will wyele doo, hym nedide to hafe wysdoṁ,
myghte, and will; þat es to say, þat he konṅ doo, and þat he

XII. may doo, and þat he wyll doo. Bot for-þi þat we hafe noghte
cunnynge, myghte, ne will of oure selfe, for-þi hase Godde gyfeṅ
vs trouthe, for to fulfill þe defaute of oure myghte. Sothefaste
lufe es for to ordayne oure will to þe tane and to þe toþer.
Trouthe ordaynes vs to Godde þe Soṅ, to whayṁ es appropyrde
Wysdoṁ; Trayste, till Godd' þe Fadyre, to whaym es appropyrde
myghte; Lufe, to þe Haly Gaste, till whayṁ es appropyrde
gudnes. And þare trouthe makes vs to hafe knawynge; and
þat knaweynge vs sayse þat He es wondyrfull; Fre es He þat

II. *St. Edmund's Mirror. Twelve Articles of the Creed.* 29

one þis manere and þus largely gyffes of His gudnes; and of þat
comes trayste, and [of] þat knawynge, þat sais þat He es gude
Commes þe thyrde Sothefastnes, þat es lufe, For ylke a thynge
4 luffes kyndely þe gude.

† Dere frende, here salt þou wyte whilke are þe twelue XIII.
artycles of þe trouthe. ¶ The firste es þis, þat Godde es ane in [† leaf 202.]
Hym-selfe and thre in *per*sou*n*s, with-owtten begynnynge, and Articles of
                                                                The twelve
                                                                the Creed.
8 wit*h*-owtten Endynge, and þat all thynges [were] made of noghte (1) God.
wit*h* His worde. ¶ Þe toþ*er* artecle es, þat Goddes son tuke (2) Christ.
flesche and blode of þe blyssed mayden Marie, and was borne of
hire, sothefaste Godd' and sothefaste man. ¶ Þe thirde es, þat He (3) His
12 was dede and grauen, noghte for nede, Bot for to by vs of His   Death.
fre will. ¶ The ferthe artecle es, þat þe same Ihesu rase fra dede (4) His Resur-
                                                                        rection.
to lyfe, and we sall ryse alswa. ¶ The fyfte artecle es, þat þe (5) His Ascen-
                                                                    sion.
same Sothefaste God and man, steighe vp in till heuen in
16 manhed and godhede; and we sall steighe vp alswa thurgh His
grace. ¶ Þe sext artecle es baptym*m*e, þat mase man clene of syn XIV.
                                                                    (6) Baptism.
þat he drawes of kynde, and gyffes grace to clense. ¶ The Seuend (7) Confirma-
artecle es confirmacion, þ*at* confermys þe Haly Gaste one man   tion.
20 þat es cristenede. ¶ Þe aughtened artecle es penance, þat duse (8) Penance.
awaye all man*er* of syn dedly and venyall. ¶ Þe nynde es þe (9) The
                                                                Eucharist.
Sacrament of þe Auter, þat co*n*fermys þe penance, and gyffes hym
force þat he fall noghte efte in syn, and vphaldes hym and
24 reconsailles hym. ¶ Þe tend' artecle es Ordyre, þat gyffes powere (10) Orders.
till þaym þat are ordeynede to do þaire Offece and to do þe
sacrament*is*. ¶ Þe elleuend' artecle es Matrimone, þat defendis (11) Matri-
                                                                    mony.
dedly syn in werke of gen*er*acyon by-twyx man and woman.
28 ¶ Þe twelfed artecle es Enoyntynge, þat men enoyntes þe seke (12) Extreme
                                                                    Unction.
in p*er*ell of dede, for alegeance of body and saule.

¶ Dere frende, aftyre sall þou wyt whilke are þe foure vertus XV.
cardynalles, thurgh whilke all manes lyfe es gou*er*nede in þis The four Car-
                                                                    dinal Vir-
32 worlde, þat es, ¶ Cunnynge and Rightwisnes, Force and Mesure. tues:
                                                                 (1) Wisdom.
Of thir foure, saise þe Haly Gaste in þe buke of Wysdom, þat (2) Right-
                                                                eousness.
þare es na thynge mare profytabill till man in erthe; and so (3) Force.
                                                              (4) Temper-
nowe, whare-fore, wha-sa walde any thynge wele do, firste hym ance.
36 byhouys þat he konn chese þe ill fra þe gude, and of twa gude, chese

II. St. Edmund's Mirror. The Seven Works of Mercy.

Prudence. þe bettire and leffe þe lesse gude; and þis es the vertu þat es callede ryghtwysnes[1]. And for-þi þat twa thynges lettes man to do wele and lefe þe yll, þat es at say, wele-fare of þis worlde, for it dessayfes hym with false vanytes; þe toþer es tribulacyon, to putt hym down with many scharpnes: agaynes wele-fare sall þou *Temperance.* hafe mesure, þat þow be noghte ouer hye. And þis vertu es *Fortitude.* called 'temperance.' And agayne aduersyte sall þou hafe 'hardynes,' þat þou be noghte casten downne. And þat vertue es callyde Force or strenght.

XVI. ¶ Here-eftyre sall þou wyte whylke are þe seuen werkes of
vij opera mercy. ¶ The firste werke of Mercy es, to gyffe mete to þe
miseri- hunngry. The toþer es, to gyffe drynke to þe thrysty. The
cordie.
The Seven thirde es, to clethe þe nakede. Þe ferthe es, to herbere þe
Works of
Mercy. herberles. Þe fyfte es, to vesete þam þat ere in prisonne.
[† leaf 202 bk.] † Þe sexte es, to comforth þe seke. The Seuend, to bery þe dede.
    Thyse are þe seuen werkes of mercy þat are langande to þe
How those body. Bot nowe may þou say to me, 'how sulde I, þat es in
that are 'in
religion' can Relygyon, and noghte hase to gyffe at ete ne at drynke, ne
perform
these. clathes to þe nakede, ne herbery to þe herberles, For I am at
oþer mens will, and noghte at myn awen? For-thi ware it better
þat I ware seculere, þat I myghte do þise werkes of mercy.'
A, dere frende, be noghte bogylode! Better it es to hafe pete
and compassione in þi herte of hym þat hase mysese and
wrechednes, Thane þou hade all þis werlde to gyffe for charyte;
For it es bettir wyth compassion to gyffe þi-selfe als þou erte,
þan it es to gyffe þat that þou hase. There-fore, dere frende,
gyffe thi-selfe; and þan gyffes þou mare þan es in all þis worlde.
Bot now may þou Say me one þis manere:—'Sothe it es þat it
es better to gyffe hym-selfe þan it es to gyffe of his, bot better
es þe tane and þe toþer þan es ane be it selfe, for lesse es a gud
The blessed- þan twa.' It es noghte swa: For whethire es better be callede
ness of
poverty. Godde, or His seruande. Thow wate wele þat es better to be
callede Godd. Bot þase þat suffirs hunngere, thryste, caulde
and defaute, and oþer wrechidnes and mysese, calles oure Lorde

---
[1] The description of the virtue of Prudence is here given to Righteousness or Justice, the account of which is omitted.

II. St. Edmund's Mirror. Riches and Poverty.

Ihesu Criste Hym-selfe; For He saise þus in þe Gosepelle, 'What als þou dyde to þe leste of myñ, þou did to me.' Saynt Barnarde says, 'Thire pure hase noghte in erthe, ne thire riche hase noghte in heueñ; and þare-fore, if þe Riche will it hafe, thaym byhoues bye it at þe pure.' Now wate I wele þou couaytes to wyte whilke are verray pure, and whilke noghte. Now herkeñ with deuocyoñ. Sum are þat hase reches and lufes thaym, and þase are þe haldande and þe couaytourse of þis worlde. Othere are þat hase þam noghte, bot thay luffe thaym, and thay walde hafe thaym gladly; and þase are þe wrechide beggers of þe worlde, and þe false folke in religyoñ, and þase are als riche and richere þan þe oþer. And of tham Ihesu saise in þe gospelle þat 'lyghtere it ware a camelle to passe thurghe a nedill eghe, þan þe riche to com in-to þe blysse of heueñ.' Sum are þat hase reches, bot thay lufe thaym noghte; Noghte for-thy þay will wele hafe þam; and þase are þe gud meñ of þe worlde þat dispendis wele that at þay hafe. Bot fone are of þase. ʒit it are oþer þat hase noghte reches, ne lufes noghte thaym, ne will noght hafe þam; and þase are þe gude folke þat are in religioñ and þase are sothefastly pure; and þairs es þe Ioye of heueñ, For þat es the benysoñ of þe pure. Than it behufes þat þe riche hafe þe reuere of þat benysoñ; and þarefore may I say, 'Blyssede be þe pouer, for þaires es þe kyngdom and þe Ioye of heueñ.' And swa may I say of þe riche, For þairs es pyne of helle. Alswa pouer þay are þat hase pouerte and lufes na reches; and pouer þay are þat hase reches and lufes pouert.

¶ Now aftire þis, awe þe to wyte whylke are þe seueñ XVII. prayers of þe *Pater noster*, þat duse away all ill and purchase all gude. And þase seueñ prayers er contende in þe *Pater noster*, þe whilke oure Lorde Ihesu Criste kennde till His discyples, how þay [suld] pray Godd þe Fadire, and said thaym one þis manere, 'When ʒe † sall praye, one þis wyese sall ʒe say, *Pater* [† leaf 203.] *noster qui es in celis, &c.*' Now, my frende, wit þou þat oure Lorde Ihesu Cryste kennes vs in þe gospelle to make þis prayere. And þare-fore I walde at þou wyste at þe begynnynge whate es prayere or orysone, and sythyñ þat þou vndirstande

What Prayer is.
þe prayere of þe *pater noster*. Prayere or Orysoñ es noghte elles bot ȝernyng of saule, with certayne trayste þat it commes þat þou prayes. And in þat trayste vs settis Ihesu Criste wheñ He kennes vs to call Godde oure fadyre þat es in heueñ, For in Hym sall man hafe certayne trayste þat He may and will all gudnes gyffe þat oure saule kañ ȝerne, and mekill mare; þe whilke es betakynde by þise wordes, *Qui es in celis*, þat es to *God, our Father.* say, þe whilke es in heueñ. For if Godde will call Hym-selfe oure fadyre, þan He makes vs to wiet þat He lufes vs als childyre, and at He will gyfe us all þat we hafe myster of. Bot certanly if all þe lufe þat euer had fadire or modire vn-to þaire childyre, or all othire lufes of þis worlde ware gedirde to-gedyre in a lufe, and ȝit þat lufe ware multipliede als mekill als mans herte moghte thynke, ȝit it moghte na thynge atteyne to þe lufe þat Godde oure fadyre hase vn-till vs, þare whare we are hys enmys. And þat sall we wele see thurgh þe grace of Godde, If we se one what manere He is oure Fadyr, and what He has doñ for vs.

Wit þou, þat wheñ God made all creaturs of noghte, we rede *He made man alone in His likeness.* noghte þat He made any creature till His lyknes bot mañ allanne; and þare-fore Godd He es, and makere of all thynges of þe worlde, Bot He es noghte þaire fadyre; Bot vn-till vs, thurghe His aweñ myghte full of mercy, es He Godd and makere and Fadyr, For þat our saule es lelly lyke vn-till þe lyknes of þe Fadyr, and þe Soñ, and þe Haly Gaste, þat ere hallyly a Godd' and persons thre. And all þis werlde He hase made to serue man, whils mane will duelle in His lele lufe als His aweñ childyre. Bot als tyte als we twyñ fra þat lele lufe, for lufe of þis lyfe, or for any oþer thynge, we losse þe lorde- chipe of þis worlde, and becommes thralles dreryly to þe deuelle, þare we ware be-fore fre, and ayers of þe erytage of þe kyngdoñ of heueñ, and to welde þe welthe of þis werlde. Allas may saye, Allas! Allas! what here es a sorowfull chaunge wha- *God's great mercy in our Creation.* sa it vndyrstode! Wit þou wele þat here es gret lykynge of lufe, when Godd þat es with-owttyñ begynnynge, and es with-owtteñ chaungeyng, and duellys with-owttyñ Endynge, for He es al-þir-myghtyeste and alþirwyseste, and alswa alþire-beste

II. St. Edmund's Mirror. God's Mercy in our Redemption.

þat manne herte may noghte thynke, in whaym es lufe and
Ioy endles, here, I say, es takyn of gret lufe, þat He deyned Hym _{God made us in His own}
to make vs till His awen lyknes righte als we had bene His _{likenes,}
_{though He}
4 awen chosen childyre, and moghte hafe lefte vs to be a littill vyle _{might have}
_{made us like}
matire als we ware made of oure modyr, þat vile es to neuen; _{beasts.}
or He moghte hafe made vs at His will anykyn oþer bestis; and
þan had we dyede to-gedire, bathe body and saule. Bot when
8 He hade made vs man, and gafe ✝ vs þe saule to His awen [✝leaf 203
bk.]
lyknes, (louede and luffede be þat Lorde!) for to be ayers of þe
Erytage of heuen and lyfe in þat gret Ioye with-owtten Ende,
Now es na herte sa herde þat it na moghte nesche, and lufe _{So our hearts}
_{ought to}
12 Swylke a Godd with all his myghte. And his herte suld melte, _{soften, and to}
_{love Him.}
filled of Ioy, if it thoghte sothely of þat grace þat oure Lorde
hase don till vs by-fore all oþer creaturs. And ȝitt did He mare
thurghe His mekill mercy; For, whene we ware, thurghe oure _{And when we}
_{were thralls to}
16 Sorowfull syn, twynnede fra Godd, oure Sweteste Fadire, and _{the evil spirit,}
_{He sent His}
become thralles to þe ill gaste, Than He, thurghe His maste _{own Son to}
mercy, Sente His awen Sonne, þat with Hym es Godd in His God-
hede, for to take flesche and blode of þe Virgyn Marie, Mayden
20 and modyr, lastand in Ioy; and one þis manere did He þe dede.
In state of thralle tuke He oure flesche to suffre þe gylteste _{take our flesh}
_{and die for us}
pouerte, and schame, and noyes, and paynnes, þat neuer dyd ill
ne na maner of syn, and Sythen delyuerde Hym till þe vileste
24 dede, and þe schamefulleste þat man moghte thynke, to delyuer
vs wreches of sorowfull handis, and of þe pynand preson puttid
in hell, and to make vs to comme till þe heghe heuen, whare _{and lift us to}
_{high heaven}
we sall be als kynges corounde in blyse, if we do þe will of þat _{and to be}
_{kings in}
28 swet Lorde, þat for vs ordeynede Hym to dye one þe crosse als _{bliss.}
þofe He had benne a wykkid thefe. Dere Frende, nowe hase
þou here twa thyngez in þe whilke Godde hase schewede vs þat
He es oure fadire, and þat He lufes vs als His awen childyre þare
32 we are agayne Hym with oure wykked syn. The firste es, þat
He made vs till His awen lyknes; and þe toþer es, þat He boghte
vs fra presoun with His precyouse dede of His manhede. For
þe fyrste, es man halden till Hym, for to lufe Hym with all his
36 herte. Bot þan may þou aske, 'what sall I do Hym for þe toþer _{What services}

II. St. Edmund's Mirror. God requires Contrition of us.

can we render unto God for His goodness?

thynge? For if I sall with pouerhede lofe Godd' þe Fadyr, and lufe Hym and serue Him with all my saule and with all my herte in all thynges, for-þi þat He made me of noghte and gafe me saule aftir His awen lyknes,—als it was commandyd in þe 4 alde lawe be-fore Godde was borne and be-com man for vs,— what moghte I now do Hym, when He, for me wrechid synnere, sa mekill Hym lawede þat He walde becomme man, and He gafe Hym to me, when He, thurghe His sweteste mercy, walde 8 dye for me, and of þe maste noyouse and þe moste vile dede þat

We cannot repay Him for His mercy.

euer was thoghte? I wate neuer what I may say here; For if I myghte lyffe a hundrethe 3ere, and if I moghte in þat tym, ilk a day at a tym, dye als vile ded als He for me dide, 3it ne ware 12 it noghte ynence His gret gyftez, when He es sothely said Goddes Sonne of heuen, and gaffe Hym selfe till vs, þat tynte was for syn thurgh, and put in to þe pyne of helle, and þare, in þe dispytte of Hym, seruede to þe deuelle. How sulde we þan 16 3elde Hym þe gude gret gyfte, when He walde sende His awen Sone to be pynede for oure syn?'

God only requires of us contrition and humility.
[† leaf 204.]

Now I sall lere the, if God gyffe me grace, how oure dere Fadir askes nane oþer store bot that we, with herte, knawe oure 20 awen Febillnes and oure wrechidnes, þat we hafe for oure awen syn. † Thane sall we be in bitternes of penance, and crye till Hym faste mercy, þat He vs saue for His haly name, For of oure selfe hafe we noghte Hym for to 3elde ; þare-fore said the 24 prophete in þe psalme, **Quid retribuam Domino pro omnibus que retribuit**[1] **michi? Calicem salutaris accipiam, et nomen Domini invocabo,** *etc'*. þat es, ' what sall I 3elde to God for all His gud gyftes þat He me gyffes als Lorde, with-owtten my 28 deserte? The coppe of hele I sall take, and calle þe name of my lorde.' The cope of hele whare-of dranke oure Lord Ihesu oure Saueour, þat es, the bytternes of þe penance in His grete pynes, and þat man in all his thoghtez calles Godez name, þat sothefastly 32 knawes þat he hase noghte of hym-selfe bot sorowe and synne.

The more we feel weak the humbler we shall be.

And wit thou þat, if sothefastenes be sett faste in thi saule, þe mare þat þou knawes þe for wrechide and febyll, þe mare sall þou

[1] MS. *retrebuit*.

II. St. Edmund's Mirror. The Duty of Brotherly Love.

meke þe, and calle on Hys mercy. And þus it was of oure swete
Lady, mayden and modyr; For scho had mare of grace þane *Such humility and meekness*
any in this lyfe, man or woman þat euer was borne, Thare-fore *as was in our Lady, should*
4 scho halde hir lesse and lawere þan any oþer wyghte, and mare *we have.*
cryede scho mercy þan any oþer man, when sothefaste Goddes
Son lighte in hir wambe. My dere frende, se now aftir-warde
why oure Lord Ihesu kennes vs in þe Gospelle to saye 'oure *What is implied by*
8 Fadire,' and noghte 'my Fadir'; For by þat will He kenn vs þat *Our Father?*
we suld gedyre all men with vs in oure prayers, For all ere oure
brethire, crystende and vncristend' men, For þat all of a gouer-
naylle hafe we a Fadyr. And þat þou may þis thynge, thurghe
12 þe grace of Godd, clerelyere See, Gyffe gude Entente till þat at
I say. Hym calles þou 'thi fleschely broþer,' þat hase his body
of þe same man and woman of whaym þou hase thyne. Thane
sall þou wele halde hym þi broþer þat hase his saule of þe Same
16 fadir of heuen of whaym þou hase þi saule, and of swylke
a kynd, and of swylke a lyknes; For als wele made Godd ilke
man till lyknes of þe Trinyte als He did þe. And þis broþer- *The duty of brotherly*
hede mare suld we lufe, and mare dere halde, þan þe broþerhede *love.*
20 of þe flesche, in als mekill als þe saule es mare nobyll þan þe
flesche, and in als mekill als Godd, oure fadir, of heuen, es
mare nobill, and mare for to lufe, þan oure fleschly fadir. And
þat suld we do if we saghe als clerely with oure gastely eghe
24 als we do with oure bodyly eghe. Bot for-thy þat we see
noghte bot with þe fleschely eghe, als it ware bestes, we hafe
na knawynge ne na lufe bot of þat broþerhede þat commes of
þe flesche stynkande and foule. **Allas!** Allas! what sorowfull
28 thynge thus hase blyndid vs! Certis, na thynge mare blyndis
manes saule þane lufe of erthely thynge þat sonne takes ende.
For-þi behufes man lefe his propire will, if he will perfitly
knawe þe lufe-somest broþerhede. Whare-of now mekill I hafe
32 spoken, For whate-sa-euer we hafe in body or in saule of
gudnes or of † fayrenes, we hafe it of oure fadyr of heuen, [† leaf 204 bk.]
Godd, þat es till vs fadir, and Euenly till all His creaturs, noghte *God the loving Father*
anely for His makynge of noghte, ne for His gouernyng of His *of all His creatures.*
36 grace, for His purchasynge þat He made of vs þat ware tynt

childir, wit*h* His flesche and His blode þat He for vs gafe, als
Saynt Austyn̄ þe nobiłł clerke witnes. He sayse ' þe Fadir
gaffe His Son̄, thurgh whaym He walde by vs thralles; He gafe
þe Haly Gaste, thurgh whaym̄ He walde purchase þe thralles 4
in His childire. Þe Sonn, He gafe in pryse of raunson̄; þe
Haly Gaste, in p*r*euelege of purchase; and þar-fore þe Fadir
kepis Hym selfe in Erytage tiłł His childir þat He purchase[d].'
And þarefore, dere frende, na man̄ sałł mystrayste of þe lufe 8

God's mercy is greater than our sin.
of His swete Fadirhede, and of His dere pete; For mare es His
mercy þan̄ ałł oure wykkednes; For wha sa calles tiłł Hym
wit*h* ałł his herte, wit*h*-owtten̄ faile He wiłł here hym̄, for He

We may therefore trustfully call upon Him.
es fułł of mercy. And þare-fore, als I be-fore saide, wit*h* ȝernynge 12
of saule and certayne trayste, calle apon̄ Hym trewely wit*h* ałł
thi herte. He es þi Fadir pereles, þat p*ur*chacecez þe pees;
and saye traystely tiłł Hym̄ als Hym-selfe vs lerede, *Pater noster
qui es in celis*, þat es to say, Oure Fadir that es in heuen̄; 16
*sanctificet*ur *nomen tuu*m, þat es to say, halyed be þi name;
*adveniat regnu*m *tuu*m, it com̄, þi kyngedom̄; *Fiat voluntas
tua, sicut in celo et in terrâ*, þi wiłł be donne, swa in erthe als it
es i*n* heuen̄; *panem nostrum cotidianu*m *da nobis hodie*, Oure 20
ylke day brede þou gyffe vs to day; *Et dimitte nobis debita
nostra, sicut et nos dimittimus debitoribus nostris*, and forgyffe
vs oure dettis als we forgyffe our dettou*r*s; *Et ne nos inducas
in temptacione*m, and suffire vs noghte be ledde in-to fandyng*is*, 24
Set libera nos a malo, bot delyuer vs fra ałł iłł thyng*es Amen*!

The Lord's Prayer passes all other prayers.
Þat es to say, Swa mot it be! Now, my dere frende, þou sałł
wyt þat þis Oryson̄ passes ałł oþer prayers, pryncypally in twa
thynges, þat es to say, in worthynes and in p*r*ofyte. In 28
worthynes, for þat God Hym-selfe mad it; and for-þi do þay gret
schame and gret vnreuerence tiłł Ih*es*u, Goddes Son̄, þat takes
þam̄ tiłł wordis ry*n*nand and curius, and leues þe prayere þat
He vs kennede, þat wate ałł þe wiłł of Godd˙ þe Fadir, and þe 32

God knows all that we wretched caitiffs need.
whilke orysone com̄mes mare tiłł His plesynge, and whate
thynges þe wrechede caytyfe hase myst*er* at pray fore. Alswa,
als I hafe sayde, He wate anely ałł þe Fadir wyłł, and He
wate ałł oure nede; and þare-fore a hundrethe thousande er 36

II. St. Edmund's Mirror. Fullness of the Paternoster.

dyssayued wit*h* multyplicati*o*ne of wordes and of orysou*n*s;
For, when þay wene þat þay hafe grete deuocyo*n*, þa*n* hafe þai
a fulle fleschely lykynge, For-thy þat ilk a fleschely lykynge
4 delytes þa*m* kyndely in swylke tu*r*nede langage ; and þare-fore *Don't delight in polisht phrases and rymes.*
I walde þat þou war warr*e*, For I say þe sykerly, þat it es a
foule lychery for to delyte þe in rym*m*es and slyke gulyardy;
ȝit one a-noþ*er* syde, Saynt Austyne, and Saynt Gregore, and
8 oþ*er* halowes þat prayede als was þaire lykynge. I blame *Those who leave the Lord's Prayer for others are to blame*
noghte prayers, bot I blame þase þat lefes þe prayere of Godd͞
þat Hym-selfe made, and lerede vs for to pray, þat es, *Pater noste*r,
and takes þa*m* tiłł þe Orysons of a synfułł Saynte whare þay
12 fynde it wrette*n*, For oure Lorde Ih*es*us Hym-selfe sayse in the
† gospełł, 'when ȝe witł praye, prayes noghte wit*h* many [†leaf 205.]
wordes, bot p*r*aye one þis manere, *Pater noste*r &c'.'

¶ Dere frende, ȝit sałł þou wit one anoþ*er* syde þat þe *Pater* *The Lord's Prayer contains all things which we need to ask.*
16 *noste*r passes ałł oþ*er* prayers in worthynes; For þare-in es
contende ałł thyngez what-sa we hafe myste*r* of, tiłł þis lyfe
or tiłł þe toþ*er*. For we p*r*aye þare-in Godd͞ þe Fadyr, þat
He delyu*er* vs of ałł illes, and þat He gyffe vs ałł gudes, and
20 þat He make vs swylke þat we may neue*r* do iłł, ne þat we may
noghte fayle of gude. And now, ałł þe iłłe þat vs greues,
ouþ*er* es it, ille þat es donne, or it es iłłe for to co*m*, or elles it
es ille þat we suffire nowe. Of þat ille þat es donne and *How we pray to be delivered from evil.*
24 passede, we praye oure swete Lorde þat He delyu*er* vs þ*er*-of,
whe*n* we say *Dimitte nobis debita nostra, etc'*. We pray Hym
delyu*er* vs of iłł þat es for to co*m*, whe*n* we say *et ne nos
inducas in temptacione*m. Of illes þat we suffire nowe, we
28 praye Hy*m* þat He delyu*er* vs, whe*n* we say *Set libera nos
a malo.* ¶ Ȝit, dere Frende, on a oþ*er* syde, wit þou þat ałł *How we pray for good.*
maner of gude þat es, Ouþ*er* it es erthely gude, or gastely gude,
or gude lastande endles. For erthely gude we praye, whe*n* we
32 saye *Panem nostrum cotidianu*m *da nobis hodie*; For gastely
gude we praye, whe*n* we say *Fiat voluntas tua, sicut in celo et in
terra*; For endles gude we praye, when we say *Adveniat regnu*m
*tuu*m; and confermy*n*g of ałł this we praye, whe*n* we say
36 *Sanctificet*ur *nomen tuu*m.

II. St. Edmund's Mirror. Lord's Prayer expounded.

¶ Now, my dere frende, þese ere seueñ prayers of þe Ewangelle þat oure Lorde Ihesu Criste kenned' tiƚƚ His dyscypiƚƚs. And þou saƚƚ wit þat þese foure wordes þat comes be-fore, þat es to wit, *Pater noster qui es in celis*, leres vs how we saƚƚ praye, 4 and what oure selfe saƚƚ be in prayere; For we saƚƚ, in ylke ane Orysoñ, haue foure thynges, þat es to say, perfite lufe tiƚƚ Hym tiƚƚ whaym we praye, and certayne trayste to haue þat at we praye fore, and stabiƚƚ trouth in Hym in whaym we trowe, 8 and sothefaste mekenes of þat, that of oure selfe, na gude we haue. Perfite lufe es vndirstandeñ in þis worde *Pater*, For ylke a creature kyndly lufes his Fadir. Certayne trayst es contende in þis worde *noster*; For if He be ours, þan may 12 we sekerly trayst in Hym þat He es haldeñ tiƚƚ vs. Stabiƚƚ trouthe es takeñ in þise wordes *Qui es*; For wheñ we say *qui es*, þan graunt we wele þat Godd' es þat we neuer sawe; and þat es ryghte trouthe, For trouthe es na noþer thyng bot 16 trowyng of thyng þat may noghte be sene. Sothefaste mekenes es betakynde in þis worde *In celis*, For when we thynke how He es heghe in Ioy, and how we are here lawe in besynes, thañ we are mekide. Bot wheñ we hafe festenede þere foure thynges 20 in oure hertes, þan may we hardyly praye, and saye with aƚƚ oure affecyoñ, *Sanctificetur nomen tuum*, þat es to say, 'haly be thi name!' als swa stabiƚƚ þi name, þat es, Fadir, in vs, þat we be one þat manere þi childire þat we do na thyng þat 24 be agaynes þi wiƚƚ, and that euer-mare we doo þat at commes to þi plesyng, thurgh grauntynge of þi grace. And for-thi þat we may noghte euer-mare do þat perfitely whyls we ere in þis caytifede worlde, þare-fore pray we þus, and sayse, *Adveniat* 28 *regnum tuum*, þat es to say, it coñ tiƚƚ vs, þi kyngdoñ, þat we regne in þe, Ihesu, in þis lyfe thurgh thi grace, and þou in vs in þe toþer lyfe thurgh Ioy. And þis ilke we praye for þase þat are in purgatorie; and for-þi þat we neuer-mare may hafe 32 † parte with Ioye of heueñ if we do noghte thi wiƚƚ in erthe, þare-fore we praye thus, *Fiat voluntas tua, sicut in celo et in terra*, þat es to say, thi wiƚƚ be doñe, als in heueñ, swa in erthe. Alswa say 'make vs to do þi wyƚƚ,' þat es to say, þou gyffe 36

II. St. Edmund's Mirror. Exposition of the Lord's Prayer.

vs grace to do all þat þou commandes, and to lefe all þat þou
defendis, and þat swa in erthe als in heuen̄, þat es to say,
als Michaelle, and Gabrielle, and Raphaelle, Cherubyn̄ and
4 Seraphyn̄, and all þe oþer angells and archangells, and all þase
þat are Ordeynede to þe endles lyfe in Ioy, in ilke a kynde,
in ilke ane ordire, and in ilke ane elde, thi wille duse; and
for-thi þat we may noghte do þi will whills we lyffe in þis body,
8 if þou ne sustayne vs noghte, þare-fore say we þus, *Panem* 'Give us this day our daily
nostrum cotidianum da nobis hodie, þat es to say, Oure ilke bread.'
day brede þou gyffe vs to-day; als swa say 'þou gyffe vs Force in
body and in saule, and hele, if it be þi will, of þe tane and offe
12 þe toþer.' And here es for to wit, þat þare es thre maners of
brede, þat es, bodyly brede, þat es to say, Fode and clethynge;
þare es brede gastely, þat es to say, of haly wrytte þe leryng;
and þare es þe brede of Eukaryste, þat es þe grace in þe
16 sacrament of þe autere, for to comforthe þe kynde of þe tane
and þe toþer.

Bot for-thi þat we ere worthi na gudnes whills we ere
bownden̄ in synn̄, þare-fore say we þus, *Dimitte nobis debita* 'Forgive us our tres-
20 *nostra, sicut et nos dimittimus debitoribus nostris*, þis es to say, passes, as we forgive them
'Forgyffe vs oure dettis als we forgyffe oure dettours.' þou sall that trespass against us.'
wyt þare oure synns byndis oure dettours to pynne; þare-fore
we pray Ihesu to for-gyff vs synnes, þat es to say, all þat we
24 hafe synnede in thoghte, in worde and in dede; and þat ryghte
als we for-gyffe till þase þat hase mysdone agaynes vs. And
for-þi þat a lyttill vs helpes to hafe forgyfnes of syn̄, if we may
noghte kepe vs fra syn̄, þare-fore pray we þus, *Et ne nos inducas* 'Lead us not into tempta-
28 *in temptacionem*, and þis es to say, 'lede us noȝte in-to na tion,'
fandyngis, als swa say, Suffere vs noghte be ouer-commen̄ in
fandyngez of þe deuell, ne of þe flesch, ne of þe werlde. And
noghte allanly we pray þat we be delyuered of all euyll
32 fandyngez, Bot alswa we pray þat we be delyuered of all ill
thyngis, when̄ we say, *Sed libera nos a malo*; and þis es to say, 'But deliver us from evil.'
'Bot delyuer vs of all ill thyngis,' þat es, of body and of saule,
of syn̄ and of pyne, For syn̄ that now es or sall be. Say we
36 Amen! þat es to say, 'swa be it!' and for-thi sayse oure Lorde

Iħesu Criste in þe gospelle, 'What sa þou prayes my fadir in my name, He sall do it;' and þer-fore say at þe Ende, *Per Dominum nostrum Iesum Cristum, filium tuum, &c'.*

And now, my dere frende, vndirstande noghte þat þou sall say þi *Pater noster* with mouthe, als I hafe it here wretyn be-fore þe. Bot say all anely þe nakede lettir with þi mouthe, and thynke in þi herte of this þat I hafe said here, of ilke a worde by it-selfe; and rekk noghte þof þou ne multyply many *Pater nosters*; For it es better to say a *Pater noster* with gude deuocyon, þan a thousande with-owtten deuocyon; For þus sais Saynte Paule appertly; he sayse, 'me ware leuer say fyve wordes in herte deuotely, þane fyve thousande † with my mouthe with-owtten lykynge.' And one þe same manere sall þou say and do at thyne offece in þe qweire; for swa sayse þe prophete, *Psallite sapienter*; and þat es to say, 'Synges and versy wyesly,' þat es, to say or to syng wyesly, þat es, þat thi herte be one þat at þou saise, and one þat at oþer saise, þat þou here it besyly; For if þi body be at thi seruyce, and þi mouthe speke one a wyse, and thi herte thynke of wrechidnes cayttfly, þan es þou twynned; For when þou swa es twynned, þou tynes þe mede of þi seruyce; For þe awe to serue Godd' with all þi herte, with all þi saule, and with all þi vertu; and swa þou may pay þi Godd. Bot þare es many thynges þat ere cause of swylke wrechede twynnynge, als mete, drynke, Reste, cleythynge, layke, discorde, Thoghte, laboure, hethynge. These makes hippynge, homerynge, of medles momellynge. And þare-fore take kepe what oure Lorde Iħesu Criste saise in þe gospelle: 'Firste,' He saise, 'sekes þe kyngdom of heuen, and all þat ȝe hafe myster of sall be gyffen ȝowe with-owttyn any askynge.'

XVIII. Thare-fore, dere Frende, þou sall wit what þou sall hafe in þe blysse of heuen. Wit þou wele þat þou sall hafe Seuen gyftes in body, and Seuen in saule, þat es to say, Fairenes in body with-owttyn fylth, lyghtenes with-owttyn slewth, Force with-owtten Feblesce, Frenes with-owtten thralledome, lykynge with-owtten noye, lufelynes with-owttyn envye, hele with-owttyn sekenes, lange lyfe with-owttyn ende. Thou sall hafe in saule, Wysedome

II. St. Edmund's Mirror. Heaven's Joys. Contemplation.

with-owtten ygnorance, Frenchipe with-owtten hateredyn, Accorde with-owtten discorde, Myghte with-owtten wayknes, honour with-owtten dishonour, Sekirnes with-owtten drede,
4 Ioy with-owtten sorowe. Bot þe wreches in helle, all þe reuerce, both in body and in saule, þat es to say, Fylth with-owttyn fairenes, Slouthe with-owtten lyghtenes, Feblesce with-owtten force, Thraldom with-owtten freenes, Angwyse
8 with-owtten lykynge, Sekenes with-owtten hele, ded with-outten ende. Thare sall be in þair saules, Ignorance with-owttyn Wysdome, hatredyn with-owtten lufe, Discorde with-owtten Accorde, feblesce with-owtten powere, Schame
12 with-owtten honour, Drede with-owtten sekernes, and Sorowe with-owtten Ioy. And for þis sall þou seke with all þi myghte, þat þou may wyn þe Ioye of heuen; For þare es sa gret Ioye and sa mekill swettnes þat, if þou myghte lyffe fra þe
16 begynnynge of þe worlde vn-till þe ende, and hafe all þe lykynge þat þou couthe ordeyne, ȝit þou sulde with gret ryghte lefe all þase for to be a day in þe Ioy of heuen. And thus endys þe toþer degre of contemplacyone, þat es to say, þe contemplacione
20 of haly writte; of þe whylke, if þou take gud kepe in þi herte, it sall be lyghte vnto þe, ilke a worde to halde. One ane oþer syde, if þou hafe mater to speke vn-to þe clerkez, be þay neuer sa wyse, or to lewede men, be þay neuer so ruyde, of þe clerkes
24 þou mofe som matirs of þis, and alswa at þou may lere more. And when þou spekes till sympill men, and ruyde, †gladly þou lere þam with swettnes, For þou hafe enoghe whare-of þou may speke, and how þou sall þi lyfe amende and gouerne, and oþer
28 menes alswa.

Þe thirde degre of contemplacyon es in Godd' Hym-selfe. XIX. And þat may be on twa maners, þat es, with-owtten in His manhede, and in His Godhede so blyschede. For þus
32 saise Saynt Austyn, For-þi be-come Godd' man, For to make mane to Se Godd' in his kynde; For wheþer som he ȝode with-in or with-owtten, euer-mare moghte man fynde pasture; with-owtten, thurgh consederacyon of His manhed'; with-in, thurghe
36 contemplacyon of His Godhede. Of His manhede sall þou thynke

[Side notes: The penalties of hell. Ills which the wretches in hell shall undergo. This is sufficient of the second part of contemplation. [†leaf 206 bk.] The third part of contemplation is of God. The manhood of Christ.]

thre thyngez: þe meknes of His Incarnacyon, þe swetenes of His conuersasion, and þe grete charite of His passione. Bot þis may þou noghte do all att anes; and þare-fore hafe I twynned the thaym by þe Seuen houres of þe daye þat þou saise in þe kyrke, Swa þat nan houre passe the, þat þou ne sall be swetely ocupyed in þi herte. Bot nowe for to do þis, þan sall þou wit þat till ilke ane houre of þe daye es dowbyll medytacyon, ane of His passyon, and anoþer of þe toþer seson. ¶ Now, dere frende, before matyns sall þou thynke of þe swete byrthe of Ihesu Cryste al-þer-fyrste, and sythyn eftyrwarde of His passion. Of His byrth, sall thou thynke besyly þe tym, and þe stede and þe houre, þat oure Lorde Ihesu Criste was borne of His modir Marie. Þe tyme was in myd-wyntter, when it was maste calde; þe houre was at mydnyghte, þe hardeste houre þat es; þe stede was in mydwarde þe strete, in a house with-owtten walles. In clowtis was He wonden, and als a chylde was He bunden; and in a crybbe by-fore ane oxe and ane asse, þat lufely lorde layde was, for þare was na noþer stede voyde. And here sall þou thynke of þe kepynge of Marye, and of hir childe, and of hir spouse Ioseph—wat Ioye Ihesu þam sente. Thou sall thynke also of þe hyrdes þat saw þe takyn of His byrthe; and þou sall thynke of þe swete felachippe of Angells, and rayse vpe thi herte and syng with þam, *Gloria in excelsis Deo, &c.* Of þe passion sall þou thynke how þat He was at swylke a tym of þe nyghte betrayed by His descyple, and taken als a traytoure, and bownden als a thefe, and ledde als a felon.

¶ Be-fore pryme þou sall thynke of þe passion of Ihesu and of His Ioyfull ryssynge. Of His passyon sall þou thynke how þe Iewes ledd Hym into þaire counsaile, and bare false wytnes agayne Hym, and put appone Hym þat He had saide blasefeme, þat es, sclandyre in Godd, and þat He had said þat He suld haue distroyede þe temple of Godd, and make agayne anoþer with-in the thirde day; and þan þay bygan to dryfe Hym till hethyng, and to fulle Hym als a fule, and spite one Hym in dispyte in His faire face; and sythyn thay hide His eghen, and gafe Hym bofetes grete, and sythen asked Hym whate He was þat Hym

II. St. Edmund's Mirror. Meditations for the 7 Hours.

smate; and sythen, þay ledde Hym dreryly to þe dede, † and ȝitt [† leaf 207.]
neuer He sayde till thaym anes why þay swa dyde. Many
othyre wykkydnes þay dide Hym, þat lange ware to telle. Ȝitt
4 before pryme sall þou thynke of þe haly rysesynge, þat at þat
tyme of þe daye Ihesu Ioyfully rase fra dede to lyfe, when
þat He hade destruyede helle and delyuerede haly sawles owte
of þe powere of þe deuelle. ¶ Ȝitt before vndrone sall þou thynke XXII.
8 of þe passion and of þe witsondaye. Of þe passion sall þou The scourging and giving of the Spirit be-fore Undroun.
thynke, how þat tyme oure Lorde Ihesu Cryste dispytousely
was dispuylede, nakkynde and bownden till a tree in Pylate
house, and swa wykkedly scourgede and doungen, þat of His
12 swete body, fra þe heued till þe fute, noghte was lefte hale. And
at þat ilke houre þou sall thynke of þe witsonnday, how þe
tym of þe day oure Lorde Ihesu Criste sente þe Haly Gaste till
His disciples, in liknes of fyre, and of tunnges, in takynnynge
16 þat þay sulde hafe abowndance in worde and brynnynge in lufe,
and þat ryghte es þe purueance of oure Lorde puruayde; For
in twa maners þe wykked gaste begylede man in paradyse, þat
es to saye, with wykked entycement of his tunge, and with þe
20 caldnes of his venym. And for-þi come þe Haly Gaste in
lyknes of tung, agayne þe Entycement of þe deuelle, and in
fyre for to distruye þe caldnes of his venym. ¶ Be-fore myddaye XXIII.
sall þou thynke of þe Anunciacyon, and of Ihesu passion. And The Annun-ciation and Crucifixion before mid-day.
24 of þe Anunciacion sall þou thynke of þe grete mercy of oure
Lorde Ihesu Criste, whi þat He walde be-comme man, and For
vs suffire þe dede in þat swete manhed' Sen He moghte hafe
boghte vs agayne on oþer manere. And þat dyde He for till
28 drawe till Hym þi luffe. For if ane hade bene þi maker, and
anoþer thi byere, and hade sufferde in thaire bodyes all oure
sorowe for to by all oure lufe, Than hade noghte oure trouthe
bene anely in ane. Off þe passion sall þou thynke at þat houre
32 how oure Lorde Ihesu was done one þe Crosse be-twyx twa
thefes, ane one His ryghte syde, and anoþer one His lefte syde,
and Hym-selfe þay hangede be-twix þam twa, alls mayster of
thefes. For if all þe sekenes of þis werlde and all þe sorowe
36 ware in þe body of a man anely, and þat man myghte consayfe

alls mekiłł noye and Angwysce and Sorowe in his body als ałł þe men of þis werlde moghte thynke, ȝitt it ware fułł littiłł or ełłs noghte to regarde of þe sorowe þat He sufferde for vs ane houre of þe daye. ¶ Before nonne sałł þou thynke of þe passion and of þe gloriouse Ascencion. Of þe passione sałł þou thynke, þat at swylke a tym of þe daye dyęde þe makere of lyfe, for þi lufe. And here sałł þou thynke of þe wordes þat Ihesu spake on þe crose, and of þe foure takynes þat be-fełłe in His dede. The fyrste worde was þis þat He spake, 'Fadire, for·gyffe þam þis syn, for þay wate noghte whate þay doo.' The toþer worde was þis, þat He said to þe thefe, 'For sothe I say the, þis day sałł þou be with me in paradyse.' The thirde was þat He saide to His modire of Sayne John His cosynne, 'Woman, lo þare thi son!' And to þe discyple saide He, 'Manne, lo þare thy Modire!' The ferthe worde þat He saide was this, 'Godd, my Godd, † whi hase þou lefte me þus.' The fyfte was, 'Scicio,' þat es to say, 'I haf thriste.' The sexte worde was this, '*In manus tuas Domine, &c*'. whilke es for to saye, 'Fadir, in-to þi haundis I gyffe my sawle.' The Seuend worde was þis, *Consummatum est*, þat es to say, 'Now es þe prophecye fulfillede,' and with þat worde He helde His hede downne, and gafe þe gaste. Now þo takynes þat ware in His dede ere þire. Firste, ałł þe erthe by-gane to tremble, and þe vaile of þe temple braste in twa and felle doun, þe stanes raue in soundire, þe graues opyned and þe dede men rase, and þe sonne with-drewe his lyghte fra þe werlde fra myddaye to noune. Of þe Ascencione sałł þou thynke that swylke a tym of þe daye wente vpe oure Lorde Ihesu Criste in-tiłł þe mounte of Olyuete, Seande His discyples and His swete modire Marie, how He steighe in-tiłł heuen, and sett Hym one Fadir righte hande; and how His dysciples turnede agayne into þe Cete, and ware in fastynge and in prayere vntiłł þe commynge of þe Haly Gaste; and þare ware togedire a hundreth and twentty in a house for to abyde þe commynge of þe Haly Gaste, als oure Lorde commande þam before. ¶ Before euensange sałł þou thynke of Ihesu passion and of His supere. Of þe passion sałł þou thynke how Ioseph

II. St. Edmund's Mirror. Meditations on the Last Supper.

of Aramathy purchaste Ihesu body of Pilate, and how þey come to þe crosse þare He hange, and þay brakke þe twa thee-banes of þe twa thefes. And þare was a knyghte redye with a spere, and perchede þe syde of Ihesu, and smate Hym to þe herte; and als sone come rynnande downe þe precyouse blode and watire. And þat was þe Rawnsone of þe whilke I be-fore spake—louede be that Lorde!—And þan Ioseph tuke Hym downe of þe crosse, for-þi þat na bodye sulde duelle on þe crosse in so hye a daye als was one þe morne. Of þe supere of Ihesu sall þou thynke, how þat tym He gafe His precyouse flesche and His blude in lyknes of brede and of wyne þat we may See; and it es sothefastely flesche and blude of Ihesu Criste, þat we may noghte See with bodyli eghen. Þe thirde thynge es gastely, þe grace þat we rescheyue when we take þat flesche and þat blude. We se þare lyknes of brede and of wyne, and it es noghte; bot we trowe þat þare es sothefastly þe flesche and þe blude of Ihesu Criste. And noghte forthi þe lyknes of flesche ne may we noghte see. And þare-fore, þare whare we sulde hafe vgglynes als vn-till oure body, for to ete flesche and drynke blude of man, Oure Lorde Ihesu Criste turnede His flesche and His blude in liknes of brede and of wyne, for to comforthe oure bodily witte thurghe swylke fude als we ere wounte for to see, and alswa for to helpe oure trouthe thurghe þat, þat we see a thynge and trowes anoþer. And þare-fore, dere frende, when þou sall gaa for to reschaife þat swete flesche and þat blude of Ihesu thi saueour, luke at þou haue verray contricyon, and repentance, and clensynge of thi syn in thi herte; For þare þou ressayfes in sacrament reghte als þou ressayfede Hym in flesche and blude—blescede be þat grace! ¶ Be-fore complyn sall þou thynke how þat Ioseph and Nicodemus wande †Ihesu body in faire schetis, and enoynte it with precyouse oynementes, and laide it in a monumente of stane, and sett þaire seles apon þe stane, and knyghtes þat sulde it kepe. The toþer thynge þat þou sall thynke in þe same tyme es þis, how Ihesus, in þe daye of supere, when He had souppede, He ȝode in-till a gardyn with His discyples, and felle downe in Orysoun, and bygann for

[side notes: the Cross and the Lord's Supper before Evensong. The Supper of the Lord. Why Christ turned His flesh and blood into bread and wine. The disposition required in us. [† leaf 208.] XXVI. Before Compline the Agony and the Burial.]

II. St. Edmund's Mirror. How God reveals Himself.

XXVII.

The contemplation of the Godhead.

to swete one swilke manere þat þe droppis of blode droppede of His blyssede face vn-tiȝt þe erthe. Now hase þou matire and manere for to thynke of Goddis manhede. And eftirwarde saȝt þou wit how þou saȝt thynke one Hym in His heghe Godhede. ¶ To þat saȝt þou wit þat Godd temperd' swa His knaweynge fra þe begynnynge of mankynde, þat He walde noghte aȝt hally schewe Hym to man̄, ne aȝt hally hele Hym̄ fra man̄. For if He hade aȝt hally schewede Hym to man̄, þan hadd' trouthe noghte bene worthe and mysbileue had noghte bene þan̄ ouercomen̄, For trouthe es of thynge þat may noghte be sene; þan þat at I see es noghte trouthe; and if He had aȝt hallily helede fra man̄, þan had trouthe noghte bene helpede, and mysbileue hade bene excusede; and for-þi þan̄ walde He in party schewe Hym̄, and in party hele Hym̄. Bot now may þou aske me, 'in how many maners He walde schewe Hym̄.'

God reveals Himself in two special manners.

I say in twa maners, ane with-in, anoþer with-owtten̄. With-in He schewede Hym̄ thurgh reuelacyon̄ and thurgh resonn̄. With-owtten̄, thurgh halye writte and thurgh creaturs.

The inward revelation of God.

Thurgh reuelacyon̄, when̄ He schewede Hym tiȝt any folke thurgh inspiracion̄ and thurghe myracle. By resonn̄, commes He tiȝt þe knawynge of man̄ one þis manere:—Ilke a man̄ may wele see in hym selfe þat at he es, and þat at he hase bene, bot he may wele wit þat he hase noghte bene ay, and for þat he wate wele þat sum̄ tym̄ he be-gan̄ for to be; þan was þaire sum̄ tym̄ when̄ he was noghte. Bot when̄ he was noghte, þan moghte he one na wyese make hym̄-selfe; and þis seghes man̄ in his creature, For he sees ilke a day sum̄ ga and sum̄ com̄,

[⌐ repeated in MS.]

Reason teaches us the eternal existence of God.

For-þi, sen̄ ilke thynges erre, and [1]þay erre noghte of[1] thaym̄ selfe, þare-fore it behoues nede þat þare be ane to gyffe aȝt thynges to be, þat es to saye of whaym alle thynges are; þare-fore it behoues of force þat He thurghe whaym alle thynges erre, be with-owtten̄ begynnynge. For if He hade begynnyng, than̄ it behoufede þat He had begynnyng of sum̄ oþer; þan̄ had He noghte bene þe first autour and þe fyrste begynnyng of aȝt thyngez. Bot þare was na thynge before Hym̄, þan he come of na noþer, þan̄ hade He neuer na begynnynge.

4

8

12

16

20

24

28

32

36

II. St. Edmund's Mirror. Why one God has Three Persons.

And þare-fore it behoufes one all maner of þe werlde, þat þare be a thynge þat neuer hade begynnynge. And when reson of man sese of force þat it may na noþer wysse be, þan he be-
4 gynnys for to trowe stabilly þat a thynge þat was with-owtten begynnynge, þat es Awtour, and makere, and gouernere of all thynges þat ere. And Hym calles men Godd' by This skill, For þis worde *Deus*, þat es to say, Godd', commes of a worde of
8 grewe þat es called *theos*, and þat es † als mekill for to say [† leaf 208 bk.]
als ane anely Godd'. And þat betakyns þis worde Godd'.

And, dere frend, þou awe to wit þat þare ne es bot a Godd', XXVIII. and þou awe to wit þat na gude may faile to Godd'. Bot for-þi And that there must be
12 þat swete thynge and gud thynge es comforthe of felaschepe, more than one Person in
þan may noghte Godd' be with-owtten gudnes of felaschipe. the Godhead.
Than be-houede it nede þat þare ware many persones in Godd',
þe hegheste gudnes. And for-þi þat felyschepe may noghte be Fellowship necessitated
16 be-twyx faere þan twa, þare-fore be-houes it be þat in Godd' two persons,
be at þe leste twa persones. And for-þi þat felyschipe es littill worthe whare þare es nan Alyance ne lufe, For-thi it behoues þat þe thirde person ware in Godd', þat ware the Alyance and
20 þe lufe be-twyx the twa. And for-þi þat anehede es gude, and manyhede alswa, þare-fore it behouede nede þat anehede and and many-hood three in
manyhede bathe ware in Godd'. And by þis skill commes man the One God.
to þe knaweynge of Godd', þat He es a Godd' in Hymselfe, and
24 thre in persones. And þis ilke may man see in hym-selfe, For he sese at þe begynnynge þat he hase in hym-selfe Powere, and sythen eftir powere he hase wysdom. And sythen be-gane he for to lufe þat wysdom; and þan begynnes he for to knawe
28 apertely þat þare es in þe saule Mighte, and of þat myghte commes wysdom, and of thayme bathe comes lufe. And when man sese þat it es one swylke manere in hym, Of þat awe hym to wit þat one swylke man awe it to be in Godd' þat es abouen
32 hym, þat es to say, þat in Godd' es myghte, and of þat commes his wysdome; and of powere and wysedom bathe comes lufe. And for-þi þat of þe fyrste personne commes þe toþer, and owte of thaym bathe comes þe thyrde, For-thi calles he þe firste The three Persons of the
36 personne Godd' þe Fadire, þe toþer Godd' þe Sonne, þe thirde Trinity.

Godd' þe Haly Gaste. And for þat it wounte to be thus in-
manges men, þat þe Fadir was mare Febill þan þe sonne, for
his elde, and þe sonne mare vnwyse þan þe Fadire for his
ȝouthe; and for þat a man sulde noghte wene þat it ware 4
swa of Godd, Tharefore es powere appropirde to Godd' þe
Fadir, wysdom to Godd' þe Sonne. And for-þi þat þis worde
Gaste sownnes sumwhate into fellenes, For-þi es swetnes, lufe,
and gudenes appropirde to þe Haly Gaste. Oppon þis maner 8
commes man firste to þe knaweynge of his Godd, how He es
with-owtten be-gynnynge, and whi He es called Godd, ane in
substance and thre in persones, and whi þe firste persone es
callede Godd' þe Fadir, þe toþer, Godd' þe Sonne, þe thyrde, 12
Godd' þe Haly Gaste; and whi powere es appropirde to Godd'
þe Fadir, and wysdom to Godd' þe Sonne, and gudnes to
Godd' þe Haly Gaste. In swylke manere sall þou knawe þi
Godd'. 16

XXIX. The fyrste degre of contemplacion es, þat þe saule be ledde
agayne to þe selfe, and gedire it all with-in þe selfe. The
toþer degre es, þat man see whate he es, swa gedyrde to-gedire.
The thirde degre es, þat he lefte hym selfe abouen hym-selfe, 20
† and payne hym for to luke one his Godd' in his awen kynde.
Bot till selfe may he neuer mare comme, vntill he hafe lerede
to resayfe ilke a bodyly ymagynacyone erthely and gastely, þat
commes to his awen herte, owþer of herynge, or of tastynge, 24
or of sweloynge, or of any oþer bodily wite, to refuse it and to
defule it, þat it may see the selfe swylke as it es with-owtten
þe bodye. Thare-fore, dere Frende, take gud hede how þe
saule es wondirfull in þe selfe, and howe it es ane in þe kynde, 28
and noghte forthi ȝit it duse dyuerse thynges; For þe selfe, it
sese þat at þou sese with thyn eghne, heris with thyne eres,
Swelawes with thi mouthe, Smelles with þi nese, and al swa þat
at þou touches with all þi membris. ¶ Thynke ȝit Eftyrwarde, 32
howe þi saule es grete, þat all anely with a thoghte it may
comprehende heuen and erthe and all þat in thaym are, if
þay ware a hundreth falde grettere þan þay are or may be.
¶ When manes lyfe es grete and swa nobill þat na creature may 36

II. St. Edmund's Mirror. God's Mercy. Life of Love.

vndirstande it perfitly, Thane grete and nobill es he þat swa nobill thynge made of noghte. He es aboueñ all thynge, and with-in all thynge, and with-owtteñ all thynge, and be-nethe
4 all thynge. He is aboueñ all thynge, all thynge gouernande, Be-nethe all thynge, berande all thynge, with-in all thynge, Fulfillande all, with-owtteñ all thynge, abowte gangande all.

¶ Swylke manere of contemplacione Engendyrs in mañ Faste
8 trouthe and sekire deuocyone. ¶ Eftir þis sall þou thynke howe *The bounty of God.* þat he es large: and þat may þou see one many maners. See at þe begynnynge howe þat he es large of erthely gude; how he gyfes his gudes als wele to þe ille als to þe gude in alle thynges
12 þat þou sese in erthe. Sytheñ eftirward' see howe þat he es large for to Forgyffe: For if a mane hym ane hade donne alls *His great mercy.* mekill ille als alle þe men of þis werlde moghte doo, ȝitt sulde he be mare redy be þe hundrethe parte for to Forgyffe hym þan
16 þat caytife sulde bee for to aske of hym forgyfenes.

¶ Nowe, my dere Frende, if þou lyfe eftir þis kennynge, þan XXX. sall þou lyfe honourabily,—and þat es þe fyrste parte of oure *This knowledge is the way to live honourably,* sermoñ þat I touchede at þe begynnynge,—and eftir þat sall
20 þou studye to lyffe lufely als to thyne euencrysteñ; and vntill *which was the first part of the Sermon.* þat sall þou sette all hally þi myghte to lufe and for to be lufede. Thou sall lufe all menne in Godd', þat es at say, anely *Next you must study to live in love.* in gudnes, and noghte for þaire fairenes of bodye for to lufe,
24 ne for force, ne for na noþer bodily vertu. For þay þat lufes in swylke manere, þay lufe noghte for Goddes sake; and for to lufe mañ in Godd' es na noþer thynge bot for to lufe hym̄ for any thynge þat may noghte be lufede with-owtteñ Godd',
28 als for gudnes or for rightewysnes, or for sothefastenes. If we do gude, þane hafe we na frende bot gude, ne nane Enemy bot ill; and þar-fore þase þat er gude sall we lufe, for-thi þat þay er gude, and þe ille sall we lufe for-þi þat þay may be gude.
32 In þis manere lufe þou na thynge bot gudnes, señ þat þou lufes all thynges for gudnes; and if þou will be lufede, schewe thi selfe lufely. Ife þou will be lufely, resayfe these thre wordes with-owtteñ forgetynge. Do þat at man biddis þe or praies *The way to shew true love.*
36 þe þat gude es; Take þat at mañ gyffes þe; and gruche noghte;

and þat at men will say þe, suffire it mekely, and wrethe the noghte. If þou lyfe þus lelely, þan lyfes thou lufely.

Dere Syster and frende, Syen eftirwarde sall þou studye for to lyffe mekely; and to þis sall þou cwn wit þat þare are twa maners of mekenes. The tane commes of sothefastenes, and þe toþer commes of charite. † By þe firste may þou hafe knaweynge of thi selfe, For thou may noghte in na manere of þis worlde see þi selfe whate þou arte in sothefastenes, if þou be noghte mekyde. The toþer manere of mekenes may þou hafe if thou thynke of þe meknes of Ihesu Criste, how þat he mekid hym þat neuer dyde syn; and swylke mekenes commes clenely of charyte.

¶ Now, my dere syster and Frende, wate þou whate it es to lyffe honourabili, lufely, and mekely; and þat es to lyffe perfitly. Now oure swete Lorde Ihesu Criste gyffe vs grace, swa Godd for to honour, and oure euencristen for to lufe, and oure selfe for to meke, þat we may for oure honourynge be honourede, and for oure lufe be lufede, and for oure mekenes be lyftede vp in-to þe heghe blysse of heuen þat he boghte vs to, Ihesu with his swete blude and his preciouse passion. Amen!

Explicit[1] speculum sancti Edmundi Cantuarensis Archiepiscopi. Dulce nomen Domini nostri Ihesu Christi: sit benedictum in secula seculorum! Amen!

[Follows, an English prose Treatise on the Lord's Prayer, 'Pater noster qui es in celis. In all the wordis þat are stabilled and sett to say in erthe,' &c.] Then comes, on leaf 211, the poem, 'Ihesu Criste, Saynte Marye sonne,' printed below, p. 79.

[1] MS. expliculum.

III. THE ABBEY OF THE HOLY GHOST.

[Robert Thornton's MS., Lincoln Cathedral Library, leaf 271.]

RELIGIO S*ancti* S*piritu*s. RELIGIO MUNDA.

OFF the abbaye of saynte Spirite, that es in a place that [leaf 271.]
es callede conscyence.

A, dere brethir and systirs! I see þat many walde be in *Because many are*
religyoñ, bot þay may noghte, owthir for pou*er*te, or for drede *hindered from actually tak-*
of thaire kyñ, or for band of Maryage; and for-thi I make *ing religious vows, he will*
4 here a buke of þe religeon of þe herte, þat es, of þe abbaye *make a book of the religion*
of the Holy Goste, that all tho þat ne may noghte be bodyly *of the heart.*
in religyoñ, þat þay may be gostely. A, Ihe*s*u, Mercy! whare
may þis abbay beste be funded, and þis religione? Now certis *The Abbey of the Holy*
8 nowhare so wele als in a place þat es called 'conscyence'; and *Ghost Consciencia.*
who so will be besy to funde þ*i*s holy religioñ, and þat may *founded in a place called*
ilke gud crystyñ mañ and woman do, þat will he besy þ*er*- *Conscience.*
abowte. And at þe begynnynge it es by-houely þat þe place
12 of thi co*n*science be clensed clene of syñ; to þe whilke clensynge
þe Haly Goste sall sende two maydyns þat ere conande: the *The maidens that cleanse*
one es callede 'rightwysnes,' and þe toþ*er* is called 'luffe of *the place, Righteous-*
clennes.' Thiese two sall cast fro þe conscience and fro þe *ness and Purity.*
16 herte, all man*er* of fylthe of foule thoghtes and desyris. Wheñ
þe place of þe conscience es wele clensed, than sall þe grownde
be mad lange and depe; and thies two maydenes sall be made,
þe one es callede 'Mekenes,' þat sall make þe grownde depe *Meekness and Poverty pre-*
20 thorowe lowlynes of hir selfe, the toþ*er* es callede 'Pou*er*te,' *pare the ground.*
þat makis it large & wyde abowne, þat castis ou*er* ylke a halfe
þe erthe owte, þat es to say, alle erthely lustes & worldely
thoghtes ferre fro þe herte, þat, if þay hase erthely gudis, wit*h*
24 luffe þay for-gete þayñ for þe tyñ, & castis no lufe to þañ,
nor hase noghte, ne settis noghte for þat tyme þaire hertes
no thynge one pañ. And thies ere called 'pure in spyrite,'
of whañ God spekes in þe gospelle, & sayse þat 'thaires es þe

III. Abbey of the Holy Ghost. The Builders of the House.

[Matt. v. 3.] kyngdom of heuen, be thies wordes *Beati pauperes spiritu,*
[* MS. rignum.] *quoniam ipsorum est regnum* ** ' cœlorum.* Blyssed es þan þat
religyon þat es funndide in pouerte and in meknes. This es
agaynes many religyous þat are couetous and prowde. 4

The Abbey built on a good river, The River of Teors. This abbaye also sall be sett on a gud reuer, and þat sall
be þe reuer of teres. For swylke abbayes þat ere sett one
swylke gude ryuers, þay are wele at ese, and þe more dylecyous
[† leaf 271 bk.] duellyng es þer. †One swylke a reuer was Mary Mawdelayne 8
fowndide, For-thy grace and rechesse come all to hir will, and
[Ps. xlv. 5.] for-thi sayde Dauid thus, *Fluminis impetus letificat ciuitatem,*
þat es to saye, 'the gude reuer mase þe Cete lykande,' for it es
clene sekyr, & ryche of all gude marchandyse. And so þe 12
reuer of teris clenses Goddis cete, þat es, mannes saule, þat
es Goddes cete. And also þe holy man sayse of fylthe of
synn, þat it brynges owte þe reches of vertus and of alle gude
thewes. And when þis grownde es made, þan sall come 16
a dameselle, Bowsomnes, on þe tone halfe, and dameselle
Obediencia. Misericordia. The walls raised by Obedience and Mercy. Miserecorde one þe toþer halfe, for to rayse þe walles one
heghte, and to make þam stalworthe, with a fre hert largely
gyfande to þe pure, & to þam þat myster hase. For when we 20
do any gud werkes of charite thorow þe grace of Gode, als
ofte sythis als we þam do in þe lufe and þe louynge of God, and
in gud Entent, als many gud stonys we laye one owre howssynge
in þe blysse of heuen, festenande togedir with þe lufe of Gode 24
Salomon. and oure euen-crysten. We rede þat Salomon made his
howssynge of gret precyouse stones. Thiese precyous stones
are almos-dedis and werkes of mercy, & holy werkes þat sall
The Love of God and right Faith are the cement. Dauid. [Ps. xxxii. 4.] be bownden to-gedir with qwyke lyme of lufe & stedfaste 28
by-leue. And for-thi sayse Dauid, *Omnia opera eius in fide,*
þat es to saye, 'alle his werkes be done in stedfaste by-leue.'
And als a walle maye not laste with-owtten syment, or more,
also no werkes þat we wyrke, are noghte worthe to God, nor 32
spedfull till oure sawles, bot þay be done in the lufe of God
Paciencia. Fortitudo. Patience and Strength shall raise the pillars. and in trewe by-leue. For alle þat þe synfull dose, alle es loste.
Sythen Dameselle Sufferance and damesell Forte sall rayse
þe pelars, & vndirsett þam so strangly, þat no wynde of wordes, 36

III. *Abbey of the Holy Ghost. Its Builders, Officers, &c.* 53

angre of stryffe, fleschely nor gastely, sowre ne swete, caste
þam̄ downe. A, dere brethir and systers, ȝitt by-houys· þe
cloystyre be made one foure corners; and it es callede 'cloyster' *Claustrum.*
4 for it closys and steskys, and warely sall be lokkede. My dere There must be a Cloister to keep from evil.
breþir and systyrs, wylke of ȝow as will halde this gastely
religyon̄, & be in ryste of sawle & in swetnes of hert, halde
þe with-in̄ þe cloyster, and so sparre þou þe ȝates, and so
8 warely kepe þou þe wardes of þi cloyster, þat no noþer fand-
yngez nor euylle styrrynges hafe in-gate in the, & make þat
thy Sylence, † and for to [   ] the, or styrre the to synn̄ [1], [†leaf 272.]
steke thyn̄ eghne fro fowle syghtes, thyn̄ heres fro foule
12 herynges, thy Mouthe fro foule speche, and thyn̄ herte fra
foule thoghtes. Scrifte sall [make] thi chapitir, Predicacion̄ *Confessio. Predicacionne.*
sall make thi fratour, Oracion̄ sall make thi chapelle, Con- *Oracio.*
templacione sall make thi dortoure, þat sall be raysede one *Shrift shall make the Chapter-house;*
16 heghte with heghe ȝernynge, and with lufe qwykkynynge to *Preaching the Fratour;*
Gode, and þat sall be owte ofe worldly noyse and of worldly *Prayer the Chapel; Con-*
angyrse and besynes, als fere furthe als þou may for þe tym̄ *templation*
thorow grace for þe tym̄ of prayere. Contemplacion̄ es a *the Dormitory.*
20 deuote rysynge of herte with byrnynge lufe to God to do wele, *Contemplacion̄.*
and in his delites Ioyes his saule, and somdele ressayues of
that swetnes þat Goddis chosen̄ childir sall hafe in heuen̄.
Rewfulnes sall make the fermorye, Deuocion̄ sall make þe *Rewfulnes. Deuocion̄.*
24 celere, Meditacion sall make the gernere. *Meditacion.*
And when all þe howses bene made, þan be-houes þe Holy *Sadness the Infirmary;*
Gaste Ordeyne þe couent of grace & of vertu. And þan sall þe *Devotion the Cellar; Meditation the Store-house.*
Holy Gaste þat þis religyone es of, bee warden̄ and visiture,
28 the whilke God þe Fadir funded thorow his powere. For þus *The Holy Ghost the Warden and Visitor.*
saise Dauide, *Fundauit eam altissimus*, and this es to saye, 'the
heghe Gode þe Fadyr Fundide this relegyone.' The Son̄
thurgh his wysedom̄ þan ordayned it, als Sayne Paule witnes *Paulus.*
32 it, *Que adeo ordinata sunt*, þat es at saye, 'alle þat es of God
the Sone, it rewlis & ordaynes.' The Holy Goste ȝemys it and
vesettes it; and þat saye [we] in holy kyrke when̄ we saye þis,

---

[1] There is some confusion in this sentence from the omission of one or more words.

III. Abbey of the Holy Ghost. Officers: Abbess Charity, &c.

Veni Creator Spiritus, with *Qui paraclitus diceris*, þat es for
to saye, 'come, þou God þe Haly Gaste, and thyne þou vesete,
Caritas. and fulfill þaɱ with grace.' And than the gude lady Charite,
Charity the Lady Abbess. als scho þat es most worthy by-fore alle oþer, sall be abbas 4
of this sely abbaye. And also, als þay þat are in relegyone
sall do no thynge, ne saye thynge, ne gange in-to no stede, ne
take no gyfte, with-owtten leue of þe abbasse. Also gastely
sall none of swylke thyngys be done with-owtten leue of charite, 8
Paulus. For thus commandes Sayne Paule, *Omnia vestra in caritate fiant*,
[1 Cor. xvi. 14.] þat es, 'what-so ʒe do, or saye, or thynke with herte, alle ʒe
mon do in charite.' A, dere breþir and systirs, whate here
es harde comandement! Bot it es noghte full ill to oure sawles 12
þat oure thoghtes & oure wordes & oure werkes be onely done
for lufe. Wayleawaye! if I durste saye! for many are in
religione, bot to fewe relegious, þat þay ne done þe comandment
[† leaf 272 bk.] of saynte Paule, or þe concelle of þe † gud lady Charite, þat 16
es abbesse of this cely relegyon. And for-thi þay lose mekill
tyɱ, and losses þaire mede, and ekes thaire payne gretly, bot
if þay amende þam, whare-fore, leue breþir and systirs, bese
euer-more wakire and warre; and in all ʒoure werkes, thynke 20
depely þat whate-so ʒee doo, be it done in þe lufe of Gode, and
Wisdom the Prioress. for þe lufe of þe lady Wysdome þat sall be prioresse; for scho
[Eccles. i. 4.] es worthi, *Nam, prior omnium creata est sapiencia*, þat es,
Wysdome. 'al-þir-firste es Wysedome made'; and thurgh þe lare of hir, 24
and þe concele of þis prioresse, sall we do alle þat we do; and
Dauid. this sayse Dauid, *Omnia in sapiencia fecisti*, þat es at saye,
[Ps. ciii. 24.] 'alle þat þou hase made, þou hase made wysely.' The gud
Mekenes the Sub-Prioress. lady Meknes þat aye Elyke makis hir selfe lowly and vndir 28
alle oþer, sall be supprioresse: hir sall ʒe honoure and wirchipe
with bouxomnes. A Ihesu! blyssede þat abbaye, and cely es
Charite. Wysedome. Mekenes. þat religyone, þat hase so haly ane abbas as Charyte, a prioresse
as Wysedome, a supprioresse as Mekenes. A, dere breþir and 32
systirs, blyssede and Cely are þay, þat es to say, those saules
are cely þat haldis þe comandment of þe abbas lady Charite,
and þe techynge of þe priores, lady Wysdome, and the concele
of þe supprioresse, lady mekenes; For who-so es bouxome to 36

III. Abbey of the Holy Ghost. Officers: Discretion, Prayer.

thir thre ladyse, and þaire lyffe rewlis aftir þaire techynge, the Fadir, the Sone, the Holy Goste, þam sall comfurthe with many gostely Ioyes, and þam helpe and socoure in alle fandinges, in angirs, þat þay ne be noghte ouercomen; þam thare drede no wrenkis ne no wylis of the fende, for why God es with þam, and standis aye by þam als a trewe kepere & a strange. And for-þi says Dauid thus, *Dominus protector vite mee, a quo* [Ps. xxvi. 1.] *trepidabo?* als if he sayd, 'God es my champyone staleworthe and trewe, þat for me, þat es so wayke and so vnmyghtfull, agaynes myn Enemyse hase vndirtane for to fyghte: whame thare me þan drede? now trewly, righte none.' We rede in a buke of Danyele þat a myghtfull was þat men callede Nabogodhonosore, þat sett in Rome thre men þat solde do & ordayne and stabyll, als baylyes, alle þe rewme, so þat þe kynge herde no noyse, ne no playnte, bot þat he myghte be in pese, & in Ioye, & in ryste in his rewme. And righte so þe rewme of þe sawle þat thiese thre baylyes are In, and þe religione þat thies thre prelates are In, þat es, Charite, Wysedome and Mekenes, thare es pese, ryste, and lykynge in saule, and comforthe in lyfe.

Damsele Discrecyone, þat es witty and be full ware, sall be tresorere; scho sall hafe in hir kepynge alle, † and ȝernely [† leaf 273.] luke þat all go wele. Orysone salle be chaunterese, þat with hertly prayers sall trauele daye & nyghte. And whate Orysone es, þe haly man sayse, *Oracio est Deo sacrificium, angelis solacium, diabolo tormentum*, þat es to saye, 'Orysone es a louely sacrafice to God, Solase and lykynge to Angells, and turment to þe fende.' It witnes in the lyfe of Saynte Barthilmewe, þat it es turment to þe fende; for þe fende cryede to hym and sayde *Bartholomee! incendunt me oraciones tue*, þat es to saye, 'Bertilmew, thi prayers byrnys me.' And þat es *meus.* lykynge to angels, Saynte Bartilmew wytnes it, and sayse, 'when we praye with deuocyone of hert, the Angels standis byfore, daunsesande & prayeande, and beris oure prayers vp, and a present of þam to þe Fadir of heuen. Þe whilke prayers oure Lorde commandes to wryte in þe buke of lyfe, þat es,

[Marginal notes:] Thou who obey Charity, Wisdom, and Meekness win God's comforting. and peace, rest, and bliss. Discretion the Treasurer. Orysone. Oryson the Chauntress. Diabolus. Bartholomeus. Angels carry our prayers up to God.

sacrafyce to God: this are of þam̅ þat hym moste payes; and
for-thi he askes vs it þer he sayse thus, *Sacrificium laudis*
[Ps. xlix. 43.] *honorificabis me*, þat es to saye, 'ʒe salle wyrchipe with

Iubilacio. sacrifice of louynge.' *Iubilacio* hir felowe sall helpe; and,
Jubilation the helper of the Chauntress. what Iubilacio̅n es, a seynt it telles, and sayse þat Iubylacio̅n
es a grete Ioye þat es consayuede in teris, thorow brynnande
luffe of spirite, þat may noghte be in all schewede, no in alle
hyde, als it fallis somtyme of tho þat God hertly lufes: þere-
eftir þat þay hafe bene in prayere and in orysone, þay ere so
lyghte & so lykande in God þat, whare-so þay go, þer hertes
synges murnynge songes of lufe-longynge to þaire lefe, þat þay
ʒerne with armys of lufe semlyly to falde, and with gastely
mourny[n]ge of his gudnes swetly to kysse, and ʒit vmwhile so
depely, þat wordis þam wanttis, for luf-longynge so ferforthe
rauesches thorow hertis, þat somtym̅ þay ne wote noghte whate

Deuocio̅n. þay do. Deuocione es celeresse, þat kepis þe wynnes, bothe þe
Devotion the Cellaress. white and þe rede, with depe vmbythynkynge of þe gudnes
of God, & of þe paynnes & of þe anguyse þat he tholede, and
of the Ioyes & þe delytes of paradyse, þat he hase ordayned

Penance. to his chose̅n. Penance sall be kychynnere, þat with grete
Penance the Cook. besynes trayuells daye & nyghte for to plese alle, and ofte
swetis with bitter teris for augyre of hir synnes. Scho makes
gud metis, þat es, many bitter sorowes alle for hir gyltez. And

[† leaf 273 bk.] † theys metis fedis þe saule, bot scho sparis hir-selfe thorow
abstynence, and etys bot littill; For, do scho neuer so mekill ne
so mony-folde of gude werkes, ay semys scho hir-selfe vnworthy

Atemper- and synfull. Atemperance seruede in the fratour þat scho to
Temperance the Waiter. ylkone so lukes þat mesure be ouer alle, þat none ouer mekill
Sobyrnes. nere ouer lyttill ete ne drynke. Sobirnes redis at þe borde
Soberness the Reader. the lyues of the haly Fadirs, and synges and rehercs whate
lyfe þat þay lede for to take gud Ensampille to do als þay dyd,

Pete. and þere thorowe slyke mede to wyn̅ als þay now hafe. Pete
Pity the Answerer. es spensere, þat dose seruesse to gud, all þat scho maye. And
Mercy. Mercy hir syster sall be ambynowre, þat gyffes to alle, and
Mercy the Almoner. Drede. noghte kane kepe to hir-selfe. The lady Drede es portere,
Dread the Porteress. þat kepis besyly þe cloyster of þe herte, & of þe conscience

III. Abbey of the Holy Ghost. Its Officers: Reason, &c.

þat chases owte alle vnthewes, and calles In alle gud vertus,
& so speres þe ȝatis of þe cloyster & þe wyndows, þat none
evylle hafe none Ingate to þe herte, thorowe þe ȝatis of þe
4 mouthe, ne thorowe þe wyndows of þe eghne, nere of þe eris.
Honeste es Maystresse of þe nouyce, and teches þam alle curtasye, *Honeste Magister*
how þay sall speke and gange, and sytt and stande, and how *Nouiciarum.*
þay sall bere þam with-owtten and with-in; howe to God, *Honesty the Mistress of the Novices.*
8 how to man, so þat alle þat þam sese, of þam may take
ensampill of alle gudnes, and alle gude thewes. Dameselle
Curtasye sall be hostelere; & þat þay comande & byddes, þat *Curtasye.*
scho sall þam resafe hendely, so þat ylke one may speke of *Courtesy and*
12 hir. And for-thi þat nowþer sall be by þam one emange the
gestes,—For it myghte falle þat dameselle Curtasye solde be oure
balde a[nd] ouer hardy,—for-thi sall scho hafe a felawe Damesele,
Symplese; for þay two alyede to-gedir thorowe felawchipe, are *Simplicity the receivers of*
16 sekyre and semande, for þe tone with-owtten þe toþer vmwhile *the guests. Why two*
es littill worthe. For ouer-grete symplesse may make of þe *receivers are needed.*
symple a sott, or ouer nyce, and ouer-grete curtasye may be
somewhile oþer to lyghte chere or to glade, or ouer-balde, for
20 to paye þe gestes; Bot fayre and wele, & with-owtten fandynge
of blame, may þay do þaire Offece both to-gedir.
Damesele Resone sall be puruerere, For scho sall ordayne *Resone.*
with-in & with owttyn so skilfully, þat þere ne be no defaute. *Reason the Purveyor.*
24 Damesele Lewte sall be fermoresse, þat sall trauelle abowte, *Service shall attend to the*
& besely serue þe seke. And for-þi sen þat in þe fermory of *hospital and nurse the*
this religyon are moo seke þan hole, mo febyll þan wighte, *sick.*
and es ouer-grete trauelle to serue þam alle hyr one, †For-thi [†leaf 274.]
28 sall scho hafe a felawe, Damesele Largesse, þat sall see full *Largitas.*
wele to ylkone after þat þam nedis. Damesele Conande and *Largess shall help her.*
Wysse, þat es callede Meditacyone, or Poleschesy, es garnere: *Poleschsy. Meditation*
scho sall gedyre and sembyll gude whete and oþer gud cornnes *the store-keeper,*
32 to-gedir, and þat fully, with grete plente, thorowe þe whilke
alle þe gud ladyse of þe howse may hafe þaire sustenance.
Meditacion es in gud thoghtes of God, & of his werkes, and *Meditacion.*
of his wordes, and of his creaturs, and of his paynnens þat *In thoughts of God.*
36 he tholede, and of his grete lufe þat he had and hase to þam

58   III. Abbey of the Holy Ghost. Its Officers: Meditation.

David had a like granary.

for whaym̄ he tholede. This garnere had þe gud kyng Dauid; For-þi was he ay riche & in plente, and for-þi he sayse in þe

[Ps. lxxi. 13.]

psaltyre, *In omnibus operibus tuis Meditabar die ac nocte*, þat es to saye, 'Lorde! in thi lawe I thynke nyghte and daye.' 4 This es begynnynge of all perfeccion̄, than̄ when̄ man̄ settis and stabyll̄s his herte in depe thynkynge on God & on his

A good thought is better than words of prayer.

werkes. For ofte es better a gud thoghte in haly meditacyon̄ þan Many wordes sayd in prayere, For þe holy thoghtes in 8 meditacion̄ cryes in Goddes eris. Ofte it falles þat þe herte es so ouer-tane and so raueschede in holy meditacyon̄, þat it wote noghte what it dose, heris, nor sayse, or seys; so depely es þe herte festenede in God and in his werkes, þat wordis 12 hym wanttis; and þe stillere þat he es in slyke Meditacion̄, the luddere he cryes in Goddes eris; and þer-fore sayd Dauid thus,

[Ps. xxxi. 3.]

Quoniam tacui dum clamarem tota die, as if he sayd, 'Lorde! lo, here, the whill̄s myn̄ herte was in depe thoghtes in the and 16 of thi werkes, it cryed one the in holy Medytacyons, and was styll̄e, as beynge domme.' And þer sayse þe glose, 'the grete cryes þat we crye to God þan, are oure grete desyres and oure grete ȝernynges.' And this sayse Saynte Denyse, þat sayse, 20 'When þe herte es lyfte and raueschede to þe lufe of God with gelouse ȝernynges, he ne may sownde with worde þat þe herte

Meditation is the Granary that keeps the wheat of Christ's body.

thynkis.' This holy Meditacione, þat es, þe gernare þat kepis ȝerely þe whete þat es rede with-owte and white with-in̄, þat 24 hase þe syde clouen̄, of þe whilke men mase gud brede, þat es called Ihesu Criste, þat with-owtten̄ was rede of his awen̄ blode, and whitte with-in̄ thorow his awen̄ mekenes and

[† leaf 274 bk.]

clennes of lyfe, and hade †his syde clouen̄ with a spere,—this 28

Sacramentum Altaris. Meditacion̄. Deuocion. Devotion the Cellarer. Pietas. Pity the Penitancer, or Pittancer.

es þe brede þat we ressayue and etis in þe Sacrament of þe altyr. And wele þou weite þat the gerner sall be abown̄ þe Selare, also sall be Meditacion̄ before deuocion̄; and for-thi meditacion̄ sall be gernare, Deuocion̄ Celerrere, and Pete pene- 32 tancere[1]. Of thiese thre sayse þe profete Dauide[2] *A Fructu frumenti vini, et olei sui, multiplicati sunt*, þat es at saye, 'Of

---

[1] Sic in MS.; but *?pittancere*, i. e. the officer who served out the rations. The Prioress had charge of the discipline.   [2] Ps. iv. 8.

III. Abbey of the Holy Ghost. Its Wheat, Wine, & Oil.

the fruyte of þe whete and wyne and oyle, þay ere fulfillede.' In þe alde lawe, in many stedis, Gode takis to his chosen thiese thre. 'Serue me,' he sayse, 'wele, & I sall gyffe ȝowe plente *The wheat, wine, and oil*
4 of whete and wyne & oyle.' Plente of whete es, hertly to *of the Abbey.*
thynke one þe croyce, and euer haffe þe passyon of Ihesu Crist *The wheat is Meditation.*
hertly in mynde. This es Meditacion. Plente of wyne, þat *The wine, Devotion.*
es þe welle of teres; wele for to wepe, this es Deuocion. *The oil is Delight in God.*
8 Plente of oyle, þat es, for to hafe delyte and sauoyre in God; and this es comforthe, for þe oyle gyffes odoure to metis, and lyghtes in þe kyrke, and byrnys in þe lampe. Also when Goddis seruandes hase depely thoghte with schire herte on
12 Gode, & on his werkes, with lufe-longynge to þam, þan hase God pete of þam, and sendis þam petance of comforthe and of gastely Ioye ; and this gyffes hym at þe begyhnyng Meditacion, and þis es þe whete þat God hyghttes vs, and deuocyone þat
16 men consaynes in medytacyon. Than sendis God sone after þe wyne, þat es, plente of teris; and after, þe wyne of swete *Virtus Vini.*
teris; than sendys he þe oyle of consolacion, þat gyffes þam *The wine is Tears; the oil, Consolation.*
Sauour, & lyghtnes his knaweliggynge, and schewes to þam of
20 his heuenly priuatyse, þat es hide fro þam þat folowes fleschely desyris, and gyffes þam selfe alle to þe wysedome of þe worlde and his fantasyse, and so enflawmes þam with þe blysse of his lufe þat þay taste somedelle, & fele how swete he es, how gud
24 he es, how luffande he es—bot noghte alle fully. I wote wele þat none may fele it fully, bot if his herte sulde bryste for lykynge of Ioye. Sayne Austyne telles of a preste þat, when *Saint Austin's story of a priest.*
he herde any thynge of God þat lykynge ware In, he wold be
28 so raueschede in Ioye þat he walde fall downe, and lygge als he ware dede. And also in þat tyme, if men layde byrnande fyre to his flesche nakide, he felid † it no more þan dose a dede [† leaf 275.]
corse. Sayne Bernarde spekes of þe wordis of Iob, þer he *Barnardus.*
32 sayse *Abscondit lucem in manibus*, þat es at say, 'God hase *Saint Bernard on the light of God.*
lyghte hyde in his handis.' Þou wote wele, he þat hase a candill lyghte by-twene his handis, he may hyde it & schewe it at his owenn will. So dose oure Lorde to his chosen.
36 When he will, he opynis his handes, and lyghtenes þam with

III. Abbey of the Holy Ghost. The Clock of the Abbey.

God gives His chosen a taste of His sweetness here.
[Ps. xxxiii. 9.]

heuenly gladnes; and when he will, he closis his handis, and withdrawes þe lykynge & þe comforthe fro þam. He wille noghte þat þay fele it fully aye, Bot here he gyffes þam as for to taste & sauour somedele how swete he es, how gud he es: als Dauid sayse, *Gustate & videte quam suauis est Dominus,* als if God sayd to vs, 'be þis comforthe and this lykynge þat þou þis schorte tym base of me, þou may taste & fele how swete, how gude I ame to my chosyn in my blysse, in þe werlde with-owtten ende'; and þus he dose, for to drawe vs fro worldly besynes, and þe lykynge þer-of, and for to enflawme oure hertes with lufe-ȝernynges, For to wyn and to hafe þe lykynge of þat Ioye, alle at þe full in body and saule, with hym for to be euer more with-owtten ende.

Jealousy shall be watcher and time-keeper.

A dameselle wyse & wele taghte, þat men calles Gelosye, þat es ay wakyre and besy euerylyke wele for to do, sall kepe þe orloge, and sall wakkyn þe oþer ladyse, & make þam arely to ryse, and go þe wyllylyere to þaire seruysse. Þer es orloges in towne þat wakyns men to ryse to bodily trauayle, & þat es þe seke; and þer es orloges in þe cete þat wakynnes þe marchauntes to wende a-bowte þaire marchandyce, þat es þe wynde þat blawes daye. And þer es orloges in religion of contemplacion. And this es of this holy relegyon þat es fundede of þe Haly Gaste, and þis es Ielosy; and this es sauoyre of perfeccion. & ofte it falles in relegion, be-fore þat þe Orloge falles or any belles rynges, Goddes gostely seruandes are lange wakenede before, and hase wepede by-fore God, and hase waschen þam with þaire teris, and þaire spyrit hase † vesete with deuote prayers and gastely comforthe. And why rose þay so arely & so tymly? Witterly for þe orloge of lufe; and damesele Ielosye had wakened þam be-fore þe tyme þat þe handmayde orloge felle. A, dere breþir and syster! sely ar tho sawles þat þe lufe of God, and longyng till hym, wakyns, and slomers noghte, no slepis noghte, in þe slowthe of fleschly lustes. For-thi he sayse in Canticis, *Ecce dormio, et cor meum vigilat*,[1] þat es at saye, 'when I slepe bodily, my flesche for

There are clocks in religion.

Before they strike, folk often rise to weep

[† leaf 275 bk.]

and pray, for damsel Jealousy woke them.

[Cant. v. 2.]

---
[1] MS. *vigelat*.

III. *Abbey of the Holy Ghost. Wicked Nuns: Envy, &c.*

to ese & ryste, my herte es ay wakyre in gelosy and in lufe-
ʒernynge to Gode.' That saule þat þus wakes to God, me
thynke hole conscyence þat werldly men thynke, and þat es
this, *Jeo ay le quer a leche, rauaylé par amours*, þat es at saye,
'Myn herte es styrte fro me, wakened with lufe.' Whate es
this þat mase þe herte fro þe flesche to wake, and for þat es it,
as it were, fremde to hym? Wittirly Ieloussye with lufe, teres,
& murnynge, with lufe-longynge consayuede in deuote vprysynge
of herte.

When this Abbaye was alle wele ordaynede, and Goddes will
seruede in ryste, & in lykynge, & in pese of saule, than come
a tyrante of þe lande thorowe his powere, and did in this holy
Abbaye Foure doghtyrs þat he hade þat were lothely & of *Quatuor filias diaboli.*
euyll maners, þat þe fende was fadyr of thiese doghtyrs. Þe Four evil damsels intro-
firste þer-of, þis foule barne-tyme, highte Envye; the toþer duced into the Abbey—
highte Pride; the thirde highte Gruchynge; the ferthe highte Envy, Pride, Grumbling,
False Demynge of oþer. Thiese foure doghetirs þan hase þe Evil-think-ing.
tyraunt, þe deuell of helle, for euyll will & malese, done in this
holy Abbaye; and þay, with þaire foule vnclennes, þe couent hase The mischief they did.
greuede and harmede, so þat þay no riste ne no pete may hafe,
nyghte nor daye, nor lykynge in saule. And when þe gud lady
Charite saw this (þat was Abbas), and the lady Wysedome (þat *Caritas.*
was prioresse), and þe lady Mekenes, supprioresse, and þe toþer *Sapiencia. Humilitas.*
gude ladyse of this holy Abbaye, that the holy Abbaye was
in poynte for to worthe to noghte thorowe þe wykkydnes † of [† leaf 276.]
thir foure, Than range [þay] þe chapetour belle, and gedirde þam
alle to-gedir, and asked concele whate was beste to do. And
than lady Dyscrecyon þam concelde þat þay solde alle falle *Discrecion.*
in prayere to þe Holy Goste, þat of this Abbay es vesetour, The counsel of Lady Dis-cretion, to
þat he haste hym for to come, as þay grete myster hade, þare pray to the Holy Ghost.
for to helpe and vesete with his grace. And þay all, at hire
consaile, with grete deuocyon of herte vnto hym, sange He, as Visitor of the Abbey
alle with a swete steuen, *Veni, creator spiritus!* And also expels the evil damsels.
sone þe Holy Goste come at þaire desyrynge, and þam com-
forthede with his grace, and chasede owte þe fowle wyghtes,
þose lothely fendis doghetirs, and clenesede þe Abbaye of all

III. *Abbey of the Holy Ghost. The Writer's Exhortation.*

Let Charity, Wisdom, and Meekness dwell in your hearts.

þe fylthe, and ordayned it, and restorede better þaɴ it was by-fore. Now I pray ȝow all in charite of God, þat all þa þat of this relegioɴ redis or heris, þat þay be bouxome wıth all þaire myghte, and suffire þat þe gud ladys be-fore namede do 4 þaire offece ilke daye gastely wıth-in þaire hertes. And luke ylkone wysely þat he ne do no trispase agayne þe rewle ne þe obedyence of þis relegioɴ, and of þase lufe-frayners. And if

If you are in sin, pray for God's help, and you shall be delivered.

thorow vnhape falle þat any of thiese foure fendis doghetirs 8 seke one any wyse any Ingate for to hafe wıth-in ȝoure hertes for to duelle, or Ingate hase wonne, and wıth ȝow duellis, do so, after þe concelle of þe lady Discrescioɴ, and gyffe ȝow to deuocioɴ wıth hertly prayers, in hope of Goddes helpe and of his socoure, 12 and ȝe sall be delyuerde thurgh þe mercy of oure Lord Ihesu Criste there. Blyssede mot he be wıth-owtteɴ ende! Ameɴ!

Explicit Relegio Sancti Spiritus. Ameɴ.

[Follows, on leaf 276, bk. 277, the Poem 'The begynnyng as of thee.']

IV. WILLIAM OF NASSINGTON'S POEM ON THE TRINITY AND UNITY, THE PASSION OF CHRIST, &c.

[430 *lines in 4-measure couplets, each couplet written as one line.*]

Incipit Tractatus Willelmi Nassyngtoñ, quondam aduocati [leaf 189.]
Iuris Eboraci, de Trinitate & Vnitate, cum declaracione operum
Dei, & de passione Domini nostri Ihesu Christi, &c.

A lord' God of myghtes maste,   *Thanksgiving*
   Fader, and Soñ, and Haly Gaste.   *to the adorable Trinity.*
   Fader, for þou ert almyghtty,
Soñ, for þou ert all wytty,   4
Haly Gaste, for thow all wyłł
That gude is, and na thynge yłł,
A God' and ane Lord' yn threhed',
And' thre persons yn anehede,   8
Thus was thow aye, and euer saił be,   *The nature of God.*
Thre yn ane, and' ane yn thre.
And begynnynge and' end of ałł thatt is,
And' þat euer was, bathe mare & lesse;   12
Begynnynge, with-outteñ begynnynge,   *He is without beginning or end.*
And' ende, with-outeñ endynge;
Thatt, be-for any thynge wer wroghtt,
Or any begynnynge was, or oghtt,   16
And' befor ałł tymes, God' was thow,
& Allmygtty & wysse, as þou ert now;
Thy myght & thy witt, of thy selfe whas tane,   [lf. 189 bk.]
For neuer God was bo[t] þou ane.   20
And ałłs þou was Gode ay suthefaste,   *God is eternal.*
Swa sałł þi Godhede euer-mare laste;

IV. *William of Nassington's Poem.*

And alls þou began all þat euer was,
Swa sall þou Ende all þat sall passe.   24
Blessed be He! Louede and blyssede ay mote þou be,
And with all my herte I thanke the,
Of all þat þou has done and wroghte,
Fra þe firste tym̄ þat þou began oghte   28
For me and for all man-kynde.
Whare-fore vs aghte ay haue þe in mynde,
We should love Him. And loue þe for [all] þou has done to mane,
Als I here, thurgh þi grace, reherse cane.   32
By God all things were made.   Fyrste, heuen̄ & erth, for man þou made,
& all þis werlde here, wyd & brade,
And al thyng þat es þer-In,
For with-owtten the es noghte bot synn,   36
The wilke was neuer thurgh the wroghte;
Þer-for in haly writt es synn̄ called noghte.
Heaven.   Heuen̄ þou made, whare þou duelles,
For oure Endles wōñny[n]ge with angells;   40
the world. And þe werlde, owre suget here to be,
To serue vs, þat we þare-In serue þe.
The firmament þou made mouande,
To noresche all thyng þare-vndire lyfande,   44
Sun, moon, and stars, &c. And the sonne, to schede þe day fra þe nyght,
And þe mone & þe sternes to tak þaire lyghte
Of þe sonne for to schyne one nyghte clere,
In takynyng þat we sall reschaife here   48
The lighte of grace, þat gastely gifte es,
Of þe, þat es sonne of ryghtwisnes.
The mone lyghte, thow made to waxe and wane,
Alls semes þat Ensample þer-by es tane,   52
Of owre lyfe, þat passes here sonne,
& waxes & wanes als lyghte of þe Monne.
The sternes þou made, on þe sky standande,
planets, all as examples to us. & the planettes, in þeire course passande,   56
For Ensaumple til vs, to knawe & se
How we sulde liffe here in ilke a degre.

IV. William of Nassington's Poem. Nature of Man.

The foure Elementës, þou mad sere,   *The four elements,*
To sustayne oure bodyly kynde here;   60
And all oþer creatoures, als was thi will,   *and all creatures,*
In sere kyndes þou made for certayn skyll;
Of wilke, som are noyeand till vs kyndly,
And som are profytable and Esye;   64
And all are they for owre profet wroghte,   *for our profit and blessing.*
Bathe they þat noyes, & þat noyes noghte.
¶ The noyeand, þou made vs for to chasty,
And to clense vs here of owre foly;   68
And to make vs, to knawe and se,
How febill, & how frele are we;
The vnnoyeand, to sustayne vs & fede,
& to helpe vs & ese vs in owre nede.   72
Thy creatours are ay whare, in sere stede,
Of whilke, som are qwyke & som are dede;   *Some things have life, some are without life.*
For som semes noghte bot als dede thynges,
Als stanes, þat has noghte bot beyngez;   76
Som, als gryse & treez þat men sese sprynge,
Has beyng & lifynge, bot na felynge.
Som, als bestes þat crepis & rynnys,
& als foghles with fethirs, & fische with fynnes,   80
Hase bathe beyng, lyffyng, & felyng,
Bot na witte ne skyll of demyng.
¶ Som, als men & Angells, has thurghe the
& thurghe þi myghte, beyng & lifyng fre,   84
And feling bath of gude and ill,
And discrecyone of witte and skylle.   *Man, the greatest work*
Thus has man beyng, als men sese,
With stanes, & lyfe with grysse & treez,   88
And felyng with bestez of sere kynde,
And with Angells skill & mynde.
Thus walde þou, are þou oghte begane,
Þat somwhat of ylke creatoure hade man.   92
Mane, thow made maste dynge creatoure,
& maste semly of schape & of stature,

God made man in His likeness.

Nota.

Therefore is he bound to love God.

[leaf 190.]

Man has a higher blessing than the other creatures, in the Redemption.

Of all oþer creatours mare or lesse,
For þou mad hym aftire thyn owen liknesse 96
And gafe hym lordechipe & powere,
Abowen all oþer vnskillwise creatures sere;
And to rewle hym with witte & skyll,
And for to knawe bathe gud & ill. 100
Whare-fore, gret lufe to man þou kide,
When þou this fore man ordaynede & dide;
It semes þou hade gret lufe tyll man,
Before are þou oghte begane. 104
¶ Lorde, I am man for whaym þou dide thus,
And þat man es ilke man & woman of vs;
And als wele all þis þou did for me,
Als for ilk man or woman þat are made thurghe the.
And for-thy þat I am þat man 109
For whaym þou al thyng begane,
I awe, thurghe ryghte, the to lufe ay,
And to loue the, bathe nyghte & daye, 112
And to wirchipe the with saule & body,
Righte als þou had donne all anely.
Lord God Almyghtty, ȝit thanke I the,
That mekill mare walde doo for me, 116
And all for man-kynd, for thy gudnes,
And thy mercy þat till vs ay redy es,
That fra heuen til erthe down walde com,
To bryng vs here owt of thraledom, 120
And of þe fendis dawngere that we ware In,
Thurghe owre foremaste fadire syn.
Lorde! mekyll þou mekede the for owre sake,
Þat come fra so heghe, owre kynde to take, 124
And vouchede-safe, swa lawe to lighte,
Þat swa heghe a lorde es of grett myghte.
Bot lufe the made, of vs mercy to haue,
Þat fra the was tynt, vs for to saue, 128
Thurghe processe of lyfe þat þou walde lede
In erthe, in oure kynde of manhede.

IV. William of Nassington's Poem. Birth of Jesus.

Firste þou lyghtede in a mayden chayste,   *God born of a Virgin.*
Þat conceyuede the of þe Haly Gaste,   132
And of hir body þat was ay wemlesse,
Thow tuke flesche & blude, & oure lyknesse,
And oure kynde here, & of nan oþer,
And be-come mane for vs, and oure brothire;   136
And, for the luffe þou hade till vs,
Walde be borne of hir, & calde Ihesus.
For Ihesus es als mekill for to saye,
Alls hele or helere, þat all hele maye.   140 *Called Jesus Saviour.*
Thow come to hele vs þat ware lorne,
Bot in na reall place þou was borne,
Nowthire in palays, castell, ne toure,
Ne in non othir stede of honoure,   144
Bot in a lawe hows; and laid þou was   *Born in lowly fashion.*
In a crybe be-fore an Oxe & an asse.
Thow wald nowthir in purpure ne byse
Be lappede, ne in nan oþer clothes of pryce,   148
Bot in vile clowttes, for to couer thi body,
For we sulde take ensample þer-by,
To lufe mekenes & gastely pouerte,
And fra reches & pompes with-draw oure herte.   152
One þe aughten day of thi byrthe here,   *Circumcised the eighth day.*
That þe firste day es of þe newe ȝere,
Circumsysede in body walde þou be,
Alls þe law was pan in sere contre.   156
In sassyng of þe lawe, and in fullfillyng,
& in Ensampill till vs, & in takenyng,
That als þou was circumsisede in body,
Swa sulde we Circumsise vs here gastely,   160
That es, we sulde schere fra vs away,
All þat til luste & likyng styre vs maye.
One the twesste day þou was vesete with kynges,
And wirchipede with thre precyous thynges,   164 *Worshipped by kings with three precious gifts.*
That es at say, with golde & Ensence,
And myre, þat þey offerde in þi presence.

| | IV. *William of Nassington's Poem. Passion of Jesus.* |

<table>
<tr><td>Meaning of the gold,</td><td>Be þe golde, may vndirstand be</td><td></td></tr>
<tr><td></td><td>That þou arte kynge of maste pouste;</td><td>168</td></tr>
<tr><td>inuense,</td><td>The Ensence þat þe was offerde nexte,</td><td></td></tr>
<tr><td></td><td>Be-takyns þat þou art souerayngne priste;</td><td></td></tr>
<tr><td>and myrrh.</td><td>The myr̄, þat kepis all thynge fra rotyng,</td><td></td></tr>
<tr><td></td><td>Be-takyns thy dede & þi beryeng.</td><td>172</td></tr>
<tr><td>At thirty years old Christ was baptized;</td><td>The thritty ȝere of þe Elde of þe,
Of Sayn Iohn wald þou bapteste be,
In þe flom̄ Iourdane specyally,</td><td></td></tr>
<tr><td></td><td>For to gyfe vs Ensample ther-by,</td><td>176</td></tr>
<tr><td></td><td>That all sulde be, þat till heuen̄ suld passe,
Baptizede in watyr als þou was;
Bot for na cause of syn̄ in the hyde,</td><td></td></tr>
<tr><td>though He never sinned.</td><td>Was þou baptizede, þat neuer syn̄ dide;</td><td>180</td></tr>
<tr><td></td><td>For In the, neuer was funden̄ gyle,
Ne nàthyng þat any saule myght fyle;
Bot for to lere vs howe we sulde begyn̄
To wesche vs of þe Origenall syn̄,</td><td>184</td></tr>
<tr><td></td><td>And for to mak vertue in all watirs to be,
For to get vs agayne with grace to be fre.</td><td></td></tr>
<tr><td>Tempted in the wilderness.</td><td>Sythen̄, when̄ þou had fasted þourghe myghte,</td><td></td></tr>
<tr><td></td><td>Fourty dayes, & fourty nyghte,</td><td>188</td></tr>
<tr><td></td><td>Thow sufferd thi selfe, temped to be,
Of þe deuell þat þare-to had leue of the,
To lere vs to wrestyll & stand styfly,</td><td></td></tr>
<tr><td></td><td>Agayne þe fandyng of þat Enmy.</td><td>192</td></tr>
<tr><td></td><td>Thow lett the, of Iudas traytour balde,</td><td></td></tr>
<tr><td>Betrayed for thirty pieces of silver.</td><td>For thritty penys to þe Iewes be saulde;
Thow lette the, alls thefe, be tane bodyly,</td><td></td></tr>
<tr><td></td><td>Of þe Iewes þat till þe hade Envye,</td><td>196</td></tr>
<tr><td></td><td>The wilke, till Anna house the ledde,
And than all thi discypills fra þe flede.</td><td></td></tr>
<tr><td>Made to suffer indignities.</td><td>Till the was don̄ thare at þe begynnyng
Many-fawlde dispyte & hethynge:</td><td>200</td></tr>
<tr><td></td><td>Firste þey spittede appon̄ þe thare,
And gafe þe many bufettes sare;</td><td></td></tr>
</table>

And thyne eghne, wiţʰ a claţʰe þey hide,
And smate þe, & askede wha it dide. 204
Siţʰen þey dide þe mare hethyng;   Sent to Herod
They lede þe to Herodes hows, þe kyng;   and Pilate.
That helde þe a fule, as hym̄ thoghte,
For þou tiłł his speche ansuerde noghte 208
He did clethe þe in whitte garment,
And til Pilate, agayne he þe sente.
Eftirwarde þou was skowreghide sare,   Scourged.
In Pilatez hows nakynde bare, 212
That thi hide was ałł to-reuen than,   [leaf 190 bk.]
And þe blude one ylke a syde down ranne.
The knyghtes, aftire þat skourgegynge,
Abowte þe lappede a mantiłł in hethynge, 216
That wiţʰ þe blude tiłł thi body cleuede;
Sythen drew þey it ofe, & þat þe greuede,
And racede of ałł þe skyne þat tyde,
For tiłł þat clethynge cleued faste þi hyde. 220
  And when þey had don þe þis payne,
They clede þe in þi awen clothyng agayne,   Crowned with
And thryste þan appon þi heuede thare,   thorns.
A Crowne of thornnes þat prykkede þe sare, 224
Of wilke þe prykkes ware swa scharpe þan,
That þey percede nere thurghe þi herne panne.
They gafe þe a rede in thi hande,   With a reed
In-stede of a ceptire, the skornande, 228   for a sceptre.
And knelide be-fore þe in hethynge,
And said tiłł þe 'haile, Iewes kynge!'
Sythen was þou demede at þe Iewes voyce,
Thurghe Pilate, to be hynged on þe croyce, 232
The wilke þou bare towarde þe stede
Whare þou was ordeynede to be don to dede.
Siţʰen was þou straynede on þe crosse so faste,   Mocked and
Thurghe þe Iewes, þat þi vaynes & synows al to-braste,   strained on the Cross.
And naylede þer-one, thurghe hand & fute, 237
For hele of my saule, & for my bute.

Crucified.	And wheñ þey had naylide þe oñ þe crosse swa,	
	They did þe aftire, strange payne & wa,	240
	For they reysede þe crosse with þi body,	
	And fychede it in a tre mortasse vyolently,	
	In wilke, þe crosse swilke a Iage tuke,	
	Þat þi body, thurghe weghte al to-schoke.	244
	Than raue thy wondes thurghe fute & hande,	
	And ware sene full wyde gapaunde,	
	And þe Ioynetes of ilk lym & bane,	
	And þe vaynes ware strydand ilkane.	248
Cries 'I thirst.'	Sitheñ þou said, hyngande oñ þe rude tree,	
	The thristede, and pañ þe Iewes bed the	
Given gall and vinegar.	A full bittire drynke, þat was wroghte	
	Of aysell & gall, þat þe lykede noghte;	252
	Neuer-þe-lattere, to taste it þou was bowñ,	
	Bot þou walde noghte swelowe it dowñ,	
	For þat thriste was noghte ells þan,	
	Bot a ȝernynge aftyre þe sawle of mañ.	256
Reproved by a thief and by Jews.	Thow suffirde many repreues þat tyde,	
	Bathe oñ þe thefe þat hange oñ þi lefte syde,	
	And of othire maysters of þe Iewry,	
	That mekill schame þe dide, & velany.	260
Cries 'Eli, Eli.'	At nonne of the daye þou cryed 'Hely,'	
	& ȝeldide þi gaste to þi fadir Almyghty.	
Dies;	Thus þou diede, to make vs free	
	Fra þe grett thraldome in whilke ware we.	264
	Bot mekill payne & mekill reprefe,	
	Þou tholed before þi dede, fore oure lufe;	
for our deliverance and example.	And noghte for to bye vs agayne anely,—	
	For why þi dede moghte suffyce vs all to bye,—	268
	Bot for we sulde þare-by Ensampill take,	
	To be pacyente in angers for þi sake,	
	And for the to thole all þat harde es,	
	Alls þou tholede for vs, thurghe þi gudnes.	272
	Ells thurte þe hafe tholede nañ oþer payne	
	Bot þe dede anely, for to bye vs agayne.	

Sythen was þou smetyn in þi reghte syde — Christ's side pierced.
With a spere, þat till þi herte gun glide, 276
Fra whilke owte rane, to oure saluacyone,
The precyous blode of owre raunsonne,
With þe water of baptym, clere & thyn,
For to wesche vs here of þe Oregynall syn. 280
¶ Lorde, for þire bitter paynes & fell,
With othire ma þat I kane tell,
That þou swa mekill suffire walde — Praise to the Saviour for his mercy.
For me synfull, þi traytoure baulde, 284
I thanke þe here Inwardly,
With all my herte and my body.
¶ A, Ihesu Crist! Lorde, full of myghte, ¶ Nota. — The unworthiness and sinfulness of man.
When I thynke, outhire day or nyghte, 288
Of swa mekill kyndnes of þe,
And of þe paynes þat þou tholide for me,
And of myn vnkyndnesse many-fawlde,
& how I to wrethe the ay hafe bene bawlde, 292
Of myn hard herte þan es grete wondire,
Þat it for sorowe bristez noghte In sundyre.
Bot flescly herte in me semes nan,
For my herte es hard als it ware stane. 296 — My heart is as hard as stone.
¶ A, Jhesu! I grante to þe my trespas,
And knawes þat I am wers þan Iudas was,
That the bytrayede als traytoure balde,
& til þe Iewes, for thritty penys sawlde. 300
For I, synfull wreche, has ofte sawlde the
For a littill worldly vanyte,
And for a littill fleschely delyte,
Whare-fore I am mare þan Iudas to wyte. 304
I halde me ȝitt werse, & mare wode
Þan þe Iewes ware þat did þe one þe rude; — Christ crucified again by sin.
For why þay dide þe bot anes þat dede,
& þey knewe þe noghte Gode in manhede; 308
And I, þat wate & knawes righte
Þat þou arte Gode ay full of myghte,

Thurghe myñ aweñ malece, as I ware wode,
Fuɫɫ ofte sythes hafe I doñ þe one þe rude.   312
For, als ofte als I hafe done dedly syñ,
And thurghe malece wetandly fallyñ there-Iñ,
Alls ofte hafe I done þe one þe rude,
In þat þat in me was, and schede þi blude.   316
  Lorde! aɫɫ if I hafe done swilke foly,
Putt me noghte away fra þi mercy,
Bot graunte me grace þat may me wysse
To amende me of þat, I hafe donne mysse;   320
Sen þat þou saide þi selfe, þou wiɫɫ noghte
The dede of synfuɫɫ þat þou has boghte,
Bot þat he turne hyɱ to doo þi wiɫɫ,
And lyfe, for þou wiɫɫ na man spyɫɫ,   324
Lorde! swylke grace þou me gyffe,
Þat I may turne me to þe, and lyffe!
  A, Lord Ihesu Criste, ȝit thanke I the,
Þat aɫɫ þis, & mare, has done for me,   328
And for saluacyone of mankynde,
For whayɱ þou was swa bitterly pynede,
And sufferde dede, als I be-for saide,
And lett þi body be in sepulcre layde.   332
  Thow ȝernede sa mekiɫɫ agayne to wyne
Aɫɫ þas þat þou hade loste for syñ,
That wheñ þow was dede, & ȝeldede þe gaste,
Als tyte tiɫɫ heɫɫ þou gun þe haste,   336
In saule & godhede, als was þi wiɫɫ,
Thy body whils in þe sepulcre lay styɫɫ;
Till þou at heɫɫ come, þou walde noghte stynte,
& ware sesede of þas þat þou hade tynte.   340
Thow spoylede heɫɫ wheñ þou come þare,
And tuke owt with the, aɫɫ þat thyne ware.
Bot þou lefte þas þare þat walde noghte trowe
In þi lawe, ne in þi biddynge bowe.   344
  Sytheñ, when þou come fra þat stede,
At þe thred day aftyre þi dede,

IV. William of Nassington's Poem. Future Judgment.

To vpe-ryse fra dede þou vouchede-safe,
To eke þe trowhe þat we here hafe,   348
And schewede the bodily in thi manhede,
To conferme þe trowthe for oure mede.
Whare-fore þi bodily vp-ryssynge,   *All men shall rise in their*
Till vs Ensample es, and takynnynge,   352 *bodies,*
That we sall ryse all generally
At þe day of dome, in saule & bodye.
Thane sall all þat are fundyñ reghtewisse,
Thurghe thyñ vprysynge, to blysse ryse;   356
Bot þay þat lyffes ill vn-to þeire Endynge,
Gettes na parte of thyñ vpe-rysynge;
Bot þay sall ryse with dule þat day,
Till þe fire of hell, þat lastes aye.   360 *and go either to Hell or*
ȝitt thi rysyng, forbyseñ till vs es,   *Bliss.*
For all þat rase fra dede til blyse Endlesse,
Swa sulde we þat til blysse will wyñ,
Gastely ryse fra dedely syñ.   364

Eftire þi rysesynge, als þe buke sais,   *Christ, risen, remained on*
Þou duellede in erthe ȝitt fourtty dayes,   *earth forty days.*
And at þe fourtty day þou stey vp-righte
Til þi fader, in-till heueñ bryghte,—   368 *Ascended into heaven.*
To teche vs þe way þat we sall wende,
Til þe gret blysse þat has nan Ende,—
And sittis þare, one þi Fadire reghte hande,
Als God & Lorde alweldande,   372
That es to saye, in Godhede eueñ
With thi Fadir & owrs in heueñ.

The tendaye aftire þat þou vp wente,   *On the tenth day after, the*
At vndrone þe Haly Gaste down þou sente   376 *Holy Ghost came down,*
Till thyñ Appostills, als þou þem hyghte,
Þat þeire hertes comforthede, & made þem lyghte,
Thurghe whame lyghtenede & leride ware we:
Off all þis, Lorde, I thankë þe.   380

A, Lorde Ihesu! at þe dredfull daye of domme,   *Christ shall come again to*
When þou sall fra heueñ come   *judgment,*

	With thyne angelɫs bryghte & clere,
	And Apostelɫs & oþer halowes sere, 384
	In þe same fourme of man, and lyknesse,
	In wilke þou was demyde here giltlesse,—
to judge the good and bad.	To deme gud & ilɫ of ilke lande,
	Schewande þi wondes al bledande, 388
	That þou walde thole for synfulɫ mane—
The strict account that must be given then.	What salɫ I say, or what salɫ I do þaṅ?
	Wheṅ alɫ oure werkes þat euer we dyde,
	Salɫ þan be schewede, & nathyng hide, 392
	Of whilke we salɫ ʒelde a-cownte straitly,
	And be demyde aftire we are worthi.
	And I, than with me na gud salɫ brynge
	Be-fore sa heghe domesmaṅ & kynge, 396
	Bot synnez þat are swa manyfaulde,
	That þey may noghte by tonge be tawlde;
	Certes I am þare-fore fulɫ dredand;
	My herte, for dred aghte to be fulɫ tremblande, 400
	Wheṅ discussione salɫ be of alɫ dedis,
	And þi wrethe salɫ be maste þat alɫ meṅ dredis.
Then can we only utter the prayer of David.	Certes I ne wate whate I may say þaṅ,
	Bot alls Dauid did, þo haly maṅ: 404
	'Do þou, Lorde, with þi seruande,
	Eftyre þi mercy, þat es ay sauande;
	And in-tilɫ dome come þou noghte
	With þi seruande þat þou has boghte.' 408
	For I hafe hade grete drede in thoghte
	Of þi domes, and þat drede leffe I noghte;
leaf 191 bk.]	For þou, Lorde, arte reghtewysse domes-mane,
	That alɫ thyng reghtewissly dem kane. 412
	And thi reghtwysse dome & reghtwyssnes
	Domes synfulɫ meṅ to payne Endlesse,
	That of þeyre wikkidnesse wilɫ noghte blyṅ,
	And þi mercy here may nott wyṅ. 416
None can be saved who has not obtained Christ's mercy here,	For sekere, of mercy nane getes he,
	In þis life bot he turne hym tilɫ þe;

IV. *Lord, Have Mercy on Me.* V. *Thanks to Christ.*

And nane may þat daye be saffe,
Bot he þi mercy in þis lyfe hafe,   420
Of whilke þou erte large & leberaṫṫ,   *which He will grant to all who ask it.*
To grante it baṫhe grete & smalle,
That mercy askes, & folowes þare-to,
And dos þare-fore þat þem̅ falles to doo.   424

Whare-fore, Lorde, sem̅ þou arte ay redy   *Lord, grant me Thy mercy now!*
To graunte tiṫṫ ilke a mam̅ þi mercy,
That sekes þar-to whils þay here lyffe,
Swilke grace in þis lyfe þou me gyffe,   428
To turne me, and to fle syn̅;
Þat I may here þi mercy wyn̅, Amen,
Thurghe whilke I may, at þe dredfuṫṫ day,
Be led to þe blyse þat saṫṫ last ay. Amen!   432

V.
THANKS TO CHRIST FOR HIS MERCIES.

[Robert Thornton's MS., Linc. Cath., on leaf 191 bk.]

Lorde Gode Ihesu cryste, Godd Almyghty,   *Christ, I thank Thee for creating me,*
   I thanke þe with aṫṫ my herte hally
     That me, man, schope and mad of noghte,
     And of vile matere me furthe broghte;   4
And my body, swa made of vile matere,
Thow knyttide to-gedire in Ioyntes sere,
And my sawle made, thurghe thyn̅ Inspayre,   *my soul,*
& gaffe me lymmes semly & faire.   8
Fra a myrke downgeom̅ þou broghte me righte,
Þat es, my modirs wambe, to þis lighte,
And Efte gate me, as þi barne newe borne thurghe baptym̅,
Þat was þe fendes childe lorne;   12
And fyve wittes of body þou has gyffem̅ me,   *and my five wits.*
And skyṫṫ, ware-with þey sulde rewlyde bee;
And aṫṫ, if I hafe done agayns þi lawe,
Thi gudes þou wiṫṫ noghte fra me drawe,   16

V. *Thanks to Christ for His Mercies.*

<small>And though I sin against Thee daily, Thou sendest me my food and clothes,</small>

That a false traytoure aganes þe es ay,
And trespes agayne the here ilke daye.
Thow sendes me here, thurghe þi purueance,
Ilke daye my nedefull sustenance,   20
That es to saye, met & clathe fre,
And all þat nedfull es to me.
Thow has tholede me, & venged þe noghte
of my synn þat I hafe agayne þe wroghte,   24
And ȝitt suffers & gyffes me space
to turne me to þe, & take þi grace;

<small>and when I have fallen in the devil's power, Thou sparest me, and hast</small>

And ay wheñ I hafe fallyn in the fendis bawndoñ,
Þou has sauede me fra fynall dampnacyon,   28
That I ware for my wikkidnes worthy;
bot þou has couerde me with þi mercy,
And ay has sparede me, & ȝitt spares,
And kepes me fra þe deuyllis snares,   32
And agayne his darttes has bene my schelde,

<small>saved me from many dangers.</small>

And has sauede me, bathe in ȝouthe & elde,
Fra many perells in many sere stedis,
And fra myschance & sudayne dedes.   36

<small>For these and all other benefits, I thank Thee, and pray Thee for Thy grace to mend my life, and live in bliss with Thee.</small>

For all thes þat I hafe rehersede here,
And for all oþer gudes & benfettes sere
That thow till me, synfull caytife,
hase gracyousely done in þis lyfe,   40
I thanke þe, Lorde, with all louyng,
And prayes þe þou take me in thi kepyng,
And saue me forthewarde as þou has done,
And graunte me þi grace, whills I here wonne,   44
To mende my lyfe, & lyfe in clennes,
Þat I may wonne with þe in blisse Endlesse. Ameñ!   46

VI. A PRAYER TO CHRIST. [on leaf 191 bk.]

(1)

Almighty God in trinite,
   Inwardly I thanke þe
   For thy gud ded þat þou me wroghte,   *God, I thank Thee for the good Thou givest me.*
And with þi precyous blude me boghte,   4
And of all gud þat þou lennes me.
Lorde, blyssede mott þou be!
Honour, Ioye & louyng
Be til þi name with-owttyn endyng! Amen!   8

(2)

Lorde God alweldande,
I beteche to-daye into þi hande,   *I commit to Thy hands myself and my friends.*
my sawle & my body,
And all my Frendes specyally,   12
Bathe þe quik and þe dede:
graunt them parte of my bede!
Kepe vs all in erthe here,—
Fore þe prayere of thi modyr dere,   16
And all thy haloghes þat are in heuen,—
Fra þe dedly synnes seuen,   *Keep us from sin,*
And fra fandyng of þe euyll wyghte,
And Fra sodayne dede, bathe daye & nyghte!   20

(3)

Schelde us fra þe paynes of hell,   *and the pains of Hell,*
þat bitter are to thole, & ffell,
And with thi grace fulfill vs all,
Þat redy we may be to þi call;   24
And late vs neuer parte fra þe,   *and let us never part from Thee!*
Alls thow for vs died one a tree!
Graunte vs, Lorde, þat [it] swa bee!
Amen! Amen, pur charite!   28

VII. A PRAYER FOR MERCY.

(1)

Jesu, have mercy on me!

[leaf 192.]

Ihesu, that diede one the rude for þe lufe of me,
  And boghte me with thi precious blode, Thow hafe
    mercy of me!
Whatt me lettes of any thyng for to luffe the,
Be it me lefe, be it me lathe, do it awaye fra me! 4

(2)

Ihesu, of whayme all trewe luffe sprynges,
  That for my lufe tholede payne,
  Till lusty lufe of erthely thynges

Let me not turn again to love of earth, but make me joy in Thy love.

    Thow thole me neuer turne agayne! 8
  In thi luffe be my likynge,
  And there-to make me glade & fayne,
  And for thy lufe to make mournynge,
    That for my lufe walde be slayne. 12
      Amen! Amen! Amen! Amen, pur charite!

[Then comes the prose treatise, 'Of the vertuȝ of the haly name of Ihesu,' printed in Hampole's Prose Treatises, E. E. T. Soc., p. 1, &c.]

VIII. FIRST HYMN TO JESUS CHRIST.

[21 alternates of 4 : *ab ab.*]

(1)   [on leaf 211.]

Ihesu Criste, Saynte Marye sonne,   Jesus!
   Thurgh whaym þis werlde was worthily wroghte,
I pray þe come, and in me wonne,   Dwell in me,
   And of all filthes clense my thoghte.   4

(2)

Ihesu Criste, my Godde verray,
   Þat of oure dere Lady was borne,
Þou helpe now, and euer and aye,   help me,
   And lat me neuer for syn be lorne!   8

(3)

Ihesu Criste, Goddes sone of heuene,
   Þat for me dyede one þe rude,
I pray þe here my symple steuene,
   Thurghe þe vertue of thi haly blude.   12

(4)

Ihesu Criste, þat one þe thirde daye,
   Fra dede to lyffe rase thurgh thi myghte,
Þou gyffe me grace the serue to paye,   give me grace,
   And þe to wirchipe, day and nyghte.   16

(5)

Ihesu, of whaym all gudnes sprynges,
   Whaym all men awe to lufe by righte,   [leaf 211, col. 2.]
Thou make me to ȝeme thi biddynges,   to fulfil thy biddings!
   And thaym fullfill with all my myghte!   20

VIII. *First Hymn to Christ.*

(6)

Ihesu Crist, þat tholede for me
Paynes & angers, bitter & felle,
<small>Let me not suffer in Hell!</small> Late me neuer be partede fra þe,
Ne thole þe bitter paynes of helle! 24

(7)

Ihesu Criste, welle of mercy,
<small>Jesus!</small> Of pete and of all gudnes,
<small>forgive my sins,</small> Of all þe synnes þat euer did I,
I pray þe gyffe me forgyffnes! 28

(8)

Ihesu, to þe I make my mane;
Ihesu, to þe I calle and crye,
Late neuer my saule with syn be slane,
For þe mekillnes of þi mercy! 32

(9)

Ihesu, þat es my saueoure,
<small>be my joy,</small> Þou be my Ioy and my solace,
My helpe, my hele, my comfortoure,
<small>[leaf 211 bk.]</small> And my socoure in ilke a place! 36

(10)

Ihesu, þat with thi blude me boghte,
<small>cleanse me,</small> Ihesu, þou make me clene of syn,
And with þi lufe þou wounde my thoghte,
And late me neuer-mare fra þe twynne! 40

(11)

Ihesu, I couayte to lufe the,
And þat es hally my 3ernynge,
Þare-fore, to lufe þe, þou lere me,
And I thi lufe sall [euer] synge. 44

(12)

Ihesu, thi lufe in-to me sende,
<small>feed me with Thy love!</small> And with þi lufe þou me Fede!
Ihesu, þi lufe ay in me lende!
Thi lufe euer be my saule mede 48

VIII. *The Soul Seeking Jesus.*

(13)
Ihesu, my herte with lufe þou lyghte!
  Thi lufe, me make euer to forsake
Aii werldly Ioy, bathe day & nyghte,
  And Ioy in þe anely to make!   52

Light my heart with love of Thee;

(14)
Ihesu, þi lufe me chaufe with-in,
  So þat na thynge bot the I seke!
In thi lufe make my saule to brynne;
  Thi lufe me make bathe milde and meke! 56

and make me meek and mild!

(15)
Ihesu, my Ioy and my louynge,
  Ihesu, my comforthe clere,
Ihesu my Godde, Ihesu my kynge,
  Ihesu withowtten pere,   60

Jesus! join

(16)
Ihesu, þat aii hase made of noghte,
  Ihesu, þat boghte me dere,
Ihesu, Ioyne þi lufe in my thoghte.
  Swa þat þay neuer be sere!   64

the love of Thee with my mind!

(17)
Ihesu, my dere, & my drewrye,
  Delyte þou arte to synge;
Ihesu, my myrthe, and my melodye,
  In-to thi lufe me brynge!   68

(18)
Ihesu, Ihesu, my hony swete,
  My herte, my comforthynge,
Ihesu, aii my bales þou bete,
  And to þi blysse me brynge!   72

Bring me to Thy bliss!

(19)
Ihesu, in thi lufe wounde my thoghte,
  And lyfte my herte to the!
Ihesu, my saule þat þou dere boghte,
  Thi lufere, mak it to bee!   76

VIII. *First Hymn to Christ.*

(20)

<small>Give me Grace,</small>　　Now, Ihesu Lorde, þou gyffe me grace,
　　　　If it be thi will,
　　　　That I may come vn-to þi place,
<small>to dwell ever with Thee !</small>　　And wonn ay with the stylle. **Amen!**　　80

Explicit Tractatus. **Explicit. Amen. Thornton. Amen.**

IX HYMN TO JESUS CHRIST AND THE VIRGIN

[13 Stanzas, 2 of 6 lines, 11 of 8: *ab ab ab ab*.]   [leaf 211 bk., col. 2.]

(1)

FADIR, and Soñ, and Haly Gaste,   *God, Three in One,*
  Lorde, to þe I make my mone,
Stedfaste kyng of myghtës maste,
  Alle-weldand Gode sittand in trone.   4
I praye þe, Lorde, þat þou þe haste
  To for-gyffe þat I hafe mysdone.   6

(2)

Lorde, hafe mercy of my syñ,   *have mercy on me!*
  And brynge me owte of all my care!   8
Euylle to doo, I couthe neuer blyñ,
  I hafe ay wroghte agaynes þi lare.
Þou rewe one me bathe owte and In,
  And hele me of my woundës sare!   12

(3)

Fadir of Heueñ, þat all may,   13
  I pray þe, Lorde, þat þou me lede,   *Lead me in the right way!*
In stabyll trouthe þe ryghtë way,
  At myñ Endynge, wheñ I sall drede.   16
Thi grace I aske, bathe nyghte & day,
  Hafe mercy now of my mysdedez!
Of myñ askynge, say me noghte nay,
  Bot helpe me, Lorde, att all my nede   20

IX. Hymn to Christ and the Virgin. Her Intercession.

(4)

Jesus! let me

Swete Ihesu þat for me was borne,
  Þou here my prayere loude and stille,
For paynes þat me ere laide beforne,
  Full ofte I syghe, and wepis my fylle,   24
Full ofte haf I bene forswourne,
  When I hafe wroghte agaynes þi will;

not be lost for my ill deeds!

Thou late me neuer be forlorne,
  Lorde, for my dedis ille!   28

(5)

Holy Ghost!

Haly Gaste, I pray to the,
  Nyghte and day with gud entente,

comfort me!

In all my sorowe þou comforthe me,
  Thi haly grace be to me sente;   32
And late me neuer bownden bee
  In dedly syn, þat I be schente,
For Marie lufe, þat mayden free,
  In whaym þou lyghtë verraymente.   36

(6)

Mary, lady!

I pray the, Lady, meke and mylde,
  Þat þou pray for my misdede,
For þe luffe of þat ilke childe,
  Þat þou saghe one þe rudë blede.   40
Ewire & ay haf I bene wylde,

[leaf 212.]

  My synfull saule es euer in drede;
Mercy, Lady, meke and mylde!

help me in my need!

  Þou helpe me euer, at all my nede!   44

(7)

Mercy, Mary, mayden clene!
  Þou late me neuer in syn duelle,
Pray for me, þat it be sene,

Shield me from the fire of Hell!

  And schelde me fra þe fyre of helle!   48
Certis, Lady, wele I wene
  Þat all my faamen may þou felle;

IX. *Man's Need of Help.*

For-þi, my sorowe to þe I mene;
    Wiþ drery mode my tale I telle.   52

(8)

Bethynke þe, Lady, euer and ay,   Mary! counsel
    Þat of women þou beris þe flour,
For synfull men, als I þe say,
    Oure Lorde hase done þe gret honour.   56
Helpe me, Lady, so wele þou may!
    Þe behouse be my consailloure;
Of consaile, Lady, I þe praye,
    And also of helpe & of socoure.   60 and help me!

(9)

Nyghte and day, in wele & wa,
    In all my sorowe, þou comforthe me,   Comfort me
And be my schelde agayne my faa;
    And kepe me, gyffe þi willes bee,   64 and keep me from sin!
Fra dedly syn þat will me slaa!
Mercy, Lady, faire and Free,
Þou take þat þe es fallen fraa,
    For thi mercy and þi pete!   68

(10)

At myn Endynge þou stand by me,   Stand by me when I die!
    Heyn when I sall founde and Fare,
When I sall qwake, and dredfull be,
    And all my synnës sowe full sare.   72
Als ay my hope hase bene in the,
    I pray þe, Lady, helpe me þare,
For þe luffe of þe swette tre,
    Þat Ihesu sprede one, his body bare.   76

(11)

Ihesu, for þat ilke hardë stounde,   Jesus! have
    Þat þou walde one þe rude tre blede,
At myne Endynge, when I sall founde,
    Hafe mercy, Lorde, of my mysdede!   80 mercy on me!

IX. Hymn to Christ and the Virgin. Prayer for Aid.

And helpe me þare of þe dedes wounde,
And kepe me þare at aff my nede!
When dede me takes, & brynges to grounde,
Lorde, þare I saff thi domës drede.   84

(12)

[leaf 212, col. 2.]
Grant me time for repentance!

For my synnes to do penance
Be-fore my dede, Lorde, graunt þou me,
And space of verray répentance
Inwardly I beseke the.   88
In thi mercy es my fyaunce,
Of my foly þou hafe peté,
And of me take þou na vengeance,
Lorde, for þi debonerte!   92

(13)

Lorde, als þou erte fuff of myghte,
Whase lufe es swetteste for to taste,
My lyfe amende, My dedis þou ryghte,
For Marie lufe, þe maydeñ chaste!   96

Bring me to the sight of Thee, God, Three in One!

And brynge me to þat ilkë syghte,
One þe to see, þare Ioy es maste,
One þe to see þat Ioyfuff syghte,
Fadir, and Sonñ, and þe Haly Gaste. Ameñ!   100

Explicit[1] &c.

[1] With a flourish like 'ff'.

X. A PRAYER TO CHRIST.

[On lf. 212, col. 2.]

Ihesu Criste, Goddes sun of heuen, kyng of kynges, and lorde of lordes, mi lorde, and my Godd! For þe mekenes of þi clene incarnacione, and thurghe þe meryte of þi harde passione, Safe vs fra dampnacione, Socoure vs in temptacione, and gyffe vs thi benysone, and of all oure wykkidnes playne perdone and full remyssione, thurgh verray contrission, nakede confessione, and worthi satisfaccione! Graunte vs alswa, Lorde Godd, in heuen ay-lastande mansione and euer to se þe cherefull visione of thi faire face, for þe lufe þat þou schewede to mankynde! Amen! *Save us from damnation, forgive our sins, and let us see thy face!*

Explicit.

[Follows, 'A [Latin] Meditacione of þe Fyve woundes of oure Lorde Ihesu Criste, with a prayere in þe same.' *Adoro te, piissime Ihesu, qui redemisti me* . . .

Then, on lf. 212 bk. col. 2, 'A [Latin] Medytacion of the Crosse of Criste, with a prayere'—*O crux frutex* . . .].

XI. MORAL POEM: WITH I. AND E.

[Eight Stanzas of 12 lines each: *ab ab* (or *cb*) *ab ab fh gh*.]

(1)

[leaf 213.]
When Adam dug, and Eve span, where was man's pride?

When Adam dalfe, and Euë spane,
Go spire, if þou may spede,
Whare was þan þe pride of man,
Þat nowe merres his mede?   4
Of erthe and lame, as was Adam,
Nakede to noye and nede,
We er, als he, maked to be,
Whills we þis lyfe sall lede.   8
With I and E, borne er we,
As Salamon vs highte,
To trauell here whills we er fere,
As fewle vn-to þe flyghte.   12

(2)

We were destined to trouble, to weal or woe.

In werlde we ware casten for care,
To we ware worthi to wende
To wele or wa, ane of þase twa,
To welde with-owtten ende.   16
For-thi, whills þou may helpe þe nowe,

Reform now!

Amend þe, & hafe mynde[1],
When þou sall ga, he bese thi Faa,
Þat here was are thi Frende.   20

[1] The ryme needs 'mende.'

XI. Moral Poem, with I. and E. Man's Perishing State.

Wit*h* E and I, I rede forthi,
Vmthynke þe ay of thre,
What we er, and whate we warre,
And whate þat we sall be.   24   *Think of what we are, were, and shall be.*

(3)

Ware þou als wysse, praysede in pryce,   *If you were as wise as*
Als was Salomon,   *Solomon,*
Wele fairere fude of bane & blude,
Þat was Absolon,   28
Strenghely and strange, to wreke thi wrang   *as strong as*
As eu*er* was Sampson,   *Sampson,*
Þou ne myghte, a day, na mare þan þay,
Þe dede wit*h*-stand allone.   32   *you couldn't resist Death.*
Wit*h* I and E, þe dede to þe,
Sall com als I þ*e* ken,
Bot þou ne wate in whatekyn state
Ne how, ne whare, ne when*n*e.   36

(4)

When bemes sall blawe, rewly one rawe,
To rekkenynge buse vs ryse,   *We must rise for Judg-*
When he sall com*m*e vn-to þat dom*m*e   *ment,*
Ih*es*u to sitt Iustyse.   40
Þat are was leue, þane mon be greue,
When all gastis sall ryse,
I say þat þan, to synfull man,
Sary bese þat assise.   44
Wit*h* I and E, he sall noghte flee,
If all he his giltes fele,
He ne may hym hide, bot þare habyde,   *and cannot hide.*
Ne fra þat dome appelle.   48

(5)

Of all thyne aughte, þat þe was raughte,
Sall þou noghte hafe, I hete,
Bot seuen fote, þare-in to rote,   *7 foot to rot in, is all we*
And a wyndynge schete.   52   *shall have.*

For-þi þou gyffe, whils þou may lyfe,
    Or all gase þat þou may gete,
Thi gaste fra Godd, þi gudes o lodde,
    Thi flesche foldes vndir fete.   56

[leaf 213 bk.]
Our executors won't care for us.

With I and E, full sekire þou be,
    Þat thynne executurs.
Of þe ne will rekke, bot skikk ande skekke
    Full baldely in thi boures.   60

(6)

To dome we drawe, þe sothe to schawe,
    In lyfe þat vs was lente.

No Latin or law can help us, Christ alone can.

No latyn ne lawe, may helpe an hawe,
    Bot rathely vs repente.   64
The croice, þe crownne, þe spere bese bowne,
    Þat Ihesu ruggede & rente ;
Þe nayles ruyde sall þe conclude
    With thyne awen argument.   68
With E, and O, take kepe þare-to,
    As Criste hym-selfe vs kende ;
We comme and goo, to wele or wo,
    That dredfull dome sall ende.   72

(7)

Of will and witt þat vesettis it
    In worde, and þat we wroghte,

We must account for all our deeds and thoughts.

Rekken we mon, and ȝelde reson
    Full rathely of our thoghte.   76
Sall no fallace cufere our case,
    Ne consaile gette we noghte ;
No gyfte ne grace, noþer þare gase,
    Bot brwke as we hafe broghte.   80
With E and I, I rede for-thi,
    Be warre nowe with thi werkes,
For terymes of ȝere, hase þou nane here,
    Thi medes sall be thi merkes.   84

(8)
What so it be, þat we here see,
Þe fairehede of thi face,   *No beauty 'll avail us,*
Thi ble so bryghte, thi mayne, thi myghte,
Þi mouthe þat myrthis mase.   88
Aíł moñ als was, to powdir passe,   *All goes in the grave.*
To graue wheñ þat þou gase,
A grysely geste, þan bese þou preste,
In armës for to brace.   92
With I and E, for leue þou me,
Bese nane, as I þe hete,
Of aíł þi kyth dare slepe þe with,   *In the grave no kinsman*
A nyghte vndir þi schete.   96 *'ll dare sleep with you.*

Sit nomen Domini benedictum, ex hoc nunc, et usque in seculum! Ameñ!

XII. A PRAYER TO JESUS.

Ihesu Criste, have mercy one me,   *[on leaf 213 bk.]*
Als þou erte kynge of mageste,   *Jesus,*

And forgiffe me my synnes aíł,   *forgive my sins, and*
Þat I hafe donne, bathe grete and smaíł,

And brynge me, if it be thi wiíł,   *bring me to heaven.*
Tiíł heueñ to wonñ ay with þe styll! Ameñ!

[Follows, 'A sermoñ þat Dañ Iohn Gaytrye made,' printed above, pp. 1–15, to the end of leaf 218 of the MS.]

XIII. A SECOND HYMN TO JESUS CHRIST.

[Thirteen Stanzas of 8 lines: *ab* (or *cb*) *ab ab ab*; and one, St. (7), of 9 lines: *ab aab ab ab*.]

(1)

[leaf 219.]
If we knew Jesus' sweetness, earthly love would be bitter.

Hesu, thi swetnes, wha moghte it se
And þare-of hafe a clere knaweynge,
All erthely lufe sulde bitter bee,
Bot thyne allane, with-owtten lesynge.   4
I pray þe, Lorde, þat lare lere mee,
Aftir þi lufe to hafe langynge,
And sadly sett my herte one þe,
In þi lufe to hafe lykynge.   8

(2)

So lykand lufe, in erthe nane es,
In saule, wha-sa couthe hertly se,
To lufe hym wele, ware mekill blysse,

He is King of Love.

For, 'kyng of lufe,' callede es he.   12
With trewe lufe, I walde, I-wysse,
So harde to hym, bownden be,
Þat my herte ware hally hys,
And oþer lufe lykede noghte me.   16

(3)

If I, for kyndnes, suld luf my kyn,
Ay me thynke þus in my thoghte,
By kyndly skyll I sulde be-gyn
At hym, þat me, gun make of noghte.   20

He has set his likeness in my soul.

Hys semblant he sette my saule with-in,
And this werlde, for me he wroghte,

XIII. *Second Hymn to Jesus Christ.* 93

 As fadir of fude, my lufe to wyne,
  For herytage in heueñ, he me boghte. 24

    (4)
 As modir, of hym̄ I may make mynde,   *He cared for*
  Þat, are my byrthe, to me tuke hede,   *me before I*
 And seyñ with baptym̄ weschede þat strynde,   *was born, He*
  With synñ was fylede with Adames dede. 28 *is my Mother,*
 With nobill mete he nureschede my kynde,
  For with his flesche he walde me fede ;
 A better fude may na mañ fynde,
  For, to lastande lyfe it will vs lede. 32

    (5)
 My broþer and syster he es by skyll,   *my Brother*
  For he saide, & lerede þat lare,   *and Sister.*
 Þat wha-sa dide his fadyr will,
  Systers and breþer till hym þay ware. 36
 My kynde also he tuke þare till ;
  Full trewly I tryste þare-fore,
 Þat he will neuer lat me spyll,
  Bot with his mercy sane my sore. 40 *He will save me.*

    (6)
 Eftyr his lufe me bude lange,
  For he has myñ, full dere boghte,[1]   [leaf 219, col. 2.]
 When I was went fra hym with wrange,
  Fra heueñ to erthë, he me soghte. 44 *He sought*
 My wrechede kynde, for me he fange,   *me from*
  And all his noblay sette at noghte ;   *Heaven, and*
 Pouerte he suffirde, & penance strange,   *suffered for me.*
  To blysse agayne are he me broghte. 48

    (7)
 Wheñ I was thralle, to make me fre,
  Mi lufe fra heueñ till erthe hym ledde,

---

[1] This line was first written thus :—
  'For he has boghte myn full dere.'

XIII. Second Hymn to Jesus Christ.

My lufe allanë, hafe walde he,
And þat my saule sulde sauede bee. 52
Þare-fore he laide his lyfe in wedde;
He fought my foe for me. With my faa, he faughte for mee;
Woundide he was, & bitterly bledde:
His precyous blude, full of plentee, 56
Full petevofely for me was schede. 57

(8)

He bled for me. ¶ His sydes full bla and bludy ware, 58
That sumtyme ware full brighte of blee,
His herte was perchede with a spere,
His bludy woundes was reuthe to see. 61
My raunson I-wys he payede þare,
He gave His life for my sin, And gaffe his lyffe for gylte of me,
His dulefull dede burde do me dere,
And perche myn herte for pure petee. 65

(9)

¶ For pete myn herte burde breke in two,
To his kyndenes, if I tuke hede;
Encheson I was, of all his wo;
He sufferde full harde for my mysdede. 69
to win me eternal Life, To lastand lyfe, for I sulde goo,
The dede he tholede in his manhede,
When his will was to lyfe also,
He rasse agayne thurghe his Godhede. 73

(10)

¶ Till heuen he wente with mekill blysse
When he hade venqwyste his bataile;
His banere full brade displayede es,
When so my faa will me assaile. 77
Wele aghte myn herte þan to be his,
For he es þat frende þat neuer will faile,
and he wants nothing but my love. And, na thynge he will I-wys,
Bot trewe lufe for his trauaile. 81

XIII. Second Hymn to Jesus Christ.

(11)

¶ Thus walde my spousë for me fyghte,   [leaf 219 bk.]
    And woundide for me, he was fułł sare,
For my lufe his dede was dyghte:
    What kyndnes myghte he do me mare?   85
To ȝelde hym his' lufe, hafe I na myghte,
    Bot lufe hym lelly, I sulde þare-fore,   And I ought to love Him loyally.
And wyrke his wiłł with werkës ryghte,
    That he me leryde with lufely lore.   89

(12)

¶ His lufly lare with werkes fulfiłł,
    Wele aghte me, wreche, if I ware kynde,   I ought to do His will,
Nyghte and daye to wirke his wiłł,
    And euer-mare hafe hym in mynde.   93
Bot gastely Enemyse greues me iłł,
    And my frele fleschë makes me blynde,   but my flesh is frail.
Thare-fore his mercy, I take me tiłł,
    For bettire bute, I kane nane fynde.   97

(13)

¶ Bettire bute es nane to me,
    Bot tiłł his mercy trewely me take,   I trust His mercy,
That with his budë made me fre,
    And me, a wreche, his sun̄ walde make.   101
I praye þat Lorde, for his pete,
    For my syn̄, noghte me for-sake,   pray for His pity.
Bot gyffe me grace, syn̄ for to flee,
    And in his lufe lat me neuer slake.   105

(14)

A, Ihesu! for þe swetnes þat in the es,   Ah, Jesu! When I die,
    Hafe mynde of me when I sałł wende!
With stedfaste trouthe my wittës wysse,
    And defende me, fra þe fende!   109   defend,

XIII. *Second Hymn to Jesus Christ.*

<small>forgive me!</small>

<small>bring me to Thy bliss.</small>

For þi mercy, forgyffe me my mysse,
  That wikkede werkes, my saule ne schende,
Bot brynge me, Lorde, vnto þi blysse,
  With þe to wonñ with-owtteñ ende. Ameñ! 113
    Explicit.

[Follows, the prose treatise on 'The Anehede of Godd with Manns Saule,' printed in Hampole's Prose Treatises, E. E. T. Soc. 1866, pp. 14–19. Then the poem 'Þi Ioy be, ilke a dele, to serue thi Godd to paye,' printed below, p. 107.]

XIV.

[*Thornton MS.*, lf. 231.]

¶ Of Sayne Iohn þe Eua*u*ngelist.

———

(Nineteen Stanzas of 14 lines each: *ab ab ab ab, ccd, ccd*.)

(1)

O F all mankynde þat he made, þat maste es of myghte,
    And of þe molde merkede and mesured that tyde,
    Wirchipede be þou Eua*u*ngelist wit*h* eu*er*-ilke a wyghte,
    Þat he wroghte in this werlde wonnande so wyde. 4
Louede be þou lufely lugede in lyghte.
    To life ay in lykynge þat lorde the relyede,
    That in Bedleme was borne of a byrde bryghte.
That barne brynge vs to blysse þare beste es to byde; 8
    To byde in his blysse,
    Thare he es, and his
      Dysciples ilkone. 11
    Whare myrthe may noghte mysse,
    That waye þou vs wysse,
      Eua*u*ngelist Iho*n*. 14

Of all men the worthiest was St. John, called of Him who was born in Bethlehem.

(2)

¶ Iohn, as þe gete or germandir gente,
    As Iasp*er* þe Iowell of gentill perry,
So was þou daynte as drowry derely endent
    In his dedis þat for dule endeynede hym to dye. 18
Þou was lufed of þat lorde þat vs lyfe lente,
Þare was na lyueande lede he lete mare by,
Ne na wyghte in þis werlde wit*h* hy*m* þat went,
And by thi werkes I wate þat þou was worthi. 22

A bright jewel among men, dearly loved of that Lord that gave us life.

XIX. Saint John. His Birth and Character.

Wele worthi þou ware,
For thi werkes ay whare,
And dedis by-dene. 25
Now forthir to fare,
Of thi mekenes mare
With mouthe will I mene. 28

(3)

Born in Galilee, of Zebedee and Mary, St. John left his father and his nets and went to Jesus.

¶ In Galylee, graythely gome was þou get,
As Godd of his gudnes graunted þe grace,
Zebede thi fadir, the fude þat the fet,
He fedd the and fosterde, þat faire was of face, 32
Þou was myldeste of mode þat euer man mett,
Thi modir highte Mary, swylk menesyng men mase.
The seet scho aste for hir sonnes myght hir thynk wele sett,
And of thaire syttynge for-sothe hafe sere solace. 36
Solace was it to þe,
The pereles of pousté
Called the full styll. 39
Þou forsuke thi fadir fre,
Schipe and nett of þe see,
And went hym vntill. 42

(4)

His mother and all his worldly goods he abandoned to follow his Lord.

¶ Thi modir, thi mobles, all maner of thyng,
Þat any man in his mynde aftir myghte mene,
Of all þe welthe & þe wanes thou hade in kepynge, 45
To cayre with þat cumly thou keste the full clene.
With þat lorde for to lende was thi lykynge,
And for his lufe all lythes lefte thou by-dene. 48
By-dene lefte þou it all,
Þat was thyne in-with walle,
The werlde þou for-suke. 51

[leaf 231, bk.]

Thare-by sett thou bot smalle
When thou com to his calle,
As witnese the buke. 54

XIV. Saint John. He was Christ's Cousin and Favourite.

(5)

¶ Thou was witty and wyse, thi werkes vn-wylde,
Þou werede the fro wyrkynges, wrechid þat ware,
Þou was methe & meke as mayden for mylde,
Thi mynde moued þou¹ fro myse one ilke a manere, 58
Thou was faire and fayntles, with na fylthe filede,
Ne with na fandyng thi flesche defoulede with na fere,
For-thi was þou chosen chaste as a child,
Oure cheftane he chose the, vnchangide of chere. 62
    Thi chere was full chaste
    Fro werkes all waste,
      Noghte assentand to syn. 65
    Full gude was thi gaste,
    Na filthe had defaste
      The verray virgyn. 68

He was wise and meek and pure and good

(6)

¶ Thow was sybbe oure saueoure, hir syster sone,
Whas semely sydis saluede oure sare,
Þat was. þe byrde so bryghte, with birdyn ȝode būn,
And þe barne alþir-beste of body scho bare. 72
Bathe frenchipe and faythe to frayste it bese fun,
In þat frely fude to folowe his fare,
For-thi with þat worthi, Iohn, wald þou wonn,
And with hym walke whate way, þat his will ware. 76
    Ware his will was to wende,
    Or hym lyked to lende,
      Bathe myldely and still, 79
    Þou helde þe ay with þat hende,
    And ferde forthe with thi frende,
      And wroghte at his wyll. 82

Akin after the flesh to the Saviour. His faithful follower in all things.

(7)

¶ Thou was preué with þat prynce in euer-ilk a place;
To the he publischede þe poyntis of his preuaté,
Firste when þat frely transfegurede his face,
To a fone of his folke, a ferly to see. 86

In the Transfiguration.

¹ *For* þe.

100 XIV. *Saint John. Care of Christ's Mother. He is tortured.*

<small>and at the Supper special grace was shewn to him.</small>

Seþen at the supere, thorghe souerayne grace,
Many selcouthe syghte schewede he to þe.
For þou was trayste and trewe, and folowede his trace,
 And tuke at his techyng, þat faythfull es and free.   90
  Free fro thralle vs to brynge,
  Heghe one rude walde he hynge,
  So lawe wald he lende.   93
 And þou, his derlyng,
 His modir in kepyng,
 To þe he be-kende.   96

(8)

<small>St. John kept the holy mother with care and duty.</small>

¶ Thou was bouxsom and bayne, hir body to tent,
 And to his byddyng bowand to blysse þat vs broghte,
Thou seruede þat semly till hir sone sent
 Aftir hir hym-selfen; and sythen þou soghte,   100

<small>After her departure, [leaf 232.] he went into Asia, and preached.</small>

In-to Asye þe way warly thou went,
 Thare worthyly werkes of wirchipe þou wroghte,
Prechide appertely the puple repent;   103
 Thorghe prikkynge of penance fra paynes þou thaym broghte;
  Þou broghte thaym to blysse
  Thorowe mendynge of mysse;
  Gret kirkes þou made.   107
 Þe Emperoure of þis
 Was warre, as I wysse,
 And hatrede he hade.   110

(9)

<small>Domitian, the heathen emperor, had him seized,</small>

¶ Domycyane, þat deuyls lymme, dedeyned at þi dede
 And demyd the, for thi doynge, with dule for to dye,
With tyrauntez he tuk the als theefe in þat thede;   113
 Thay toylede the by-twene thaym, and threted the thraly.
Thase licherouse lurdans, laytheste in lede,
 To PorteLatyn thase laddes the ledden full laythely;
Thane the boustoure balde, with barett he bedde
 That thay thi body suld bare, with bale for to bye.   118

XIV. Saint John. He is banished, but returns to Ephesus.

    To by was þou made bare,
    And done in a tonñ thare, *and boiled in oil; then laid*
    With oyle wellande hate. 121
    Seþeñ wald þay noghte spare;
    Þay sett the full sare *on an iron plate.*
    One ane yreñ plate. 124

(10)

Of all þe dedes þay couthe doo, þat derfe ware & dill, *But no tortures could*
Thou dyede noghte, for thaire dede dide no dere vn-to the; *hurt him.*
Foulely foullede þay thi flesche, ȝit felid þou nane ille,
For-thi þi fameñ the flemede owte of cuntre. 128 *Therefore he was banished to Patmos, where he wrote the Apocalypse.*
Þan to Pathmos, a place, passede þou vn-tyll,
The Apocalips in that place, with a peñ free
Wysely þou wrate it, with witt and with will;
And for thi werke þou ware worthi wirchipede to be. 132
    To be wirchiped with myghte,
    Þou ware worthi full ryghte
    In euer-ilk a place. 135
    Thou was witnes of lyghte,
    That wysses euer-ilk a wyghte
    Thi name es Goddes grace. 138

(11)

Grete grace was þe gyffeñ & grauntede also,
Thurghe His gudnes, þat gyfes vs all gyftes of mayne:
Whils þou suggeourned in þat suyle, Domycyane, thi foo, *But Domitian being slain,*
At a semle, þat segge, in certayne was slayne. 142
Þan þou gysed the gerne, and gafe þe to goo
Till Ephesyñ graythely þe gates þat ware gayne. *St. John returned to Ephesus, where he was joyfully received.*
Feele folke ware thi frendes þare þou ferde froo,
And for to frayste of thi fare, þe toþer ware fayne. 146
    Fayne ware þe folke free,
    And come rynnande to the,
    And hailsed the hame. 149
    And saide þus vn-to the,
    'Blissede ay mote he be,
    Þat commes in Goddes name!' 152

XIV. Saint John. The Miracles he works.

(12)

[leaf 232, bk.]
He raised Drucyane to life.

Thane was Drucyane dede, thi derlynge so dere,
And sulde to delfynge be done, dredles, þat daye,
Bot þou bade thayme habyde, and sett down þe bere,
Then blyssede þe body, bare þare it laye.   156
Scho sett hir vp softely with a blythe chere,
Als scho hade slepede, it semede, sothe for to saye;

Many folk followed St. John.

Þay hade wondir of þat wyghte, þe wyes þat þere ware,
And all wirchipede thi werke, þat wente by þe waye.   160
By þe way þay þat went,
Þay lefte landis and rent,
With the for to wende;   163
To no thyng tuke þay tent,
And sone sum of thaym repent,
By fondyng of þe fende.   166

(13)

He turned sticks into gold, and made precious stones.

Þay ware cumbyrde in couetyse, þe caytefs had care,
For þaire knaues ware cledde in clethyng full clene,
And þay hade no thyng in hande as þay had hadde are,
And ware noghte halden so myghty as þay had are bene;
For-thi wroghte þou þaire will: of wandes þat ware,   171
Thow made golde full gude, and gafe þam, I wene;
Smale stanes of þe see, saynede þou þare,   173
And þay warre saphirs; for-sothe was nane swylke sene.
Sene swylke was þare none,
For fyne precyouse stone.
The wandes when þou badde,   177
Þay ware golde ylkone:
Þou gafe thaym welthe mare wone
Þan þay euer hadde.   180

(14)

He raised a child to life,

When þay had welthe more wane þan þay euer bewanne,
Þay wente home: by þe waye, vnwysely þay wroghte.
A ȝonge barne in þat burghe was dede ryghte thane;
Þat ilke body þat hym bare, to bale scho was broghte.   184

XIV. *Saint John. Poison does not hurt him.* 103

His modir come murnande, with hir many mane:
To the made thay thayre mane, mele myghte thay noghte;
And for thay grett so grysely, to grete þou bygane;
   To Godd, of his gudnes, seþen þou besoghte;   188
   Þou besoghte Godd of myghte;
   Þan þe childe rase vpe-ryghte,
   And tolde þam full euen   191 who testified against the
   Þat lett by þi lare lyghte,   lovers of gold.
   And couetede þe golde bryghte,
   How þay hadd loste heuen.   194

(15)

Than thay wepede and weryede þaire werke and þaire wyll, The gold-lovers did
Þat þay, for welthe of þe werlde, sulde wende vn-to woo; penance, and the gold and
Thow said, 'will ȝe suffire sothely and still   precious stones turned
Seuen dayes penance ?' and sonne said thay 300.   198 back again.
Thay tuke at thi techynge, and traysted þar-tyll;
Þay had for-thynkyng in thoghte, þat þay it fledde froo.
Þe precyouse stones semly to see appon syll,
And þe golde in thaire kynde, a-gayne gun þay goo. 202
   Thay go agayne in degre   [leaf 233.]
   As þaire kynde was to bee,
   Stones as þay ware.   205
   The golde turnede to wandis free;
   Þan þat syghte fra thay see,
   Myse didd þay na mare.   208

(16)

In þat cuntre was a clerke knawen and kende,   A cunning clerk called
Þay callede hym Craton þe cunande, thurghe-owte clergy, Craton opposed St.
All þe lande and þat lede þat he gun in lende,   John, and tried to poison
With his lawes and his lare warre þay ledd by; 212 him.
Þat philosophir, all þe folke faste he defende
That thay suld noghte in thi faythe, Iohn, þam affy.
Þus merrede he þe men, þaire mysse for to mende,
And thurghe mawmetis he made mon a maystry. 216

XIV. Saint John. *He bids folk love others as themselves.*

Thurgh thaym, the he soghte;
For the, Iohn, forsothe he wroghte,
A puysoñ to profe the. 219
He saide, as he thoghte,
'If it noyede the noghte,
Þañ walde he lufe the.' 222

(17)

The poison slew two prisoners, but St. John restored them, and drank the cup without harm.

Bot þat puysoñ to profe, that prouddeste in palle,
Profirde it two presoners, was puneschede in pyne,
Als faste als þay felyd it, downe dede guñ þay falle,
So was it felt for to frayste, þe fylthe was so fyne. 226
Bot þou sanede thaym̄ alsone, seande thaym alle,
And saynede þe coppe owtely, and suppede it off syne;
Thow hade no harme: þat be-helde þat hendeste in hall,
And to the hally þay heledide, bathe he and his hyne.
His hyne holly, and he,
Trewely trowede þare to þe,
Be-come þare thi brothire. 233
Þou said to þat menȝe,
'Luke þat ȝe lufande be,
Ilkone to oþer.' 236

(18)

He preacht brotherly love and charity.

Thou bade thaym be free to frayste in þaire fare,
Faythefull and frendely till euerilk a fere,
'What may þis mene' quod these meñ, 'mone it vs mare;
We hafe no mencyoñ ne mynde of þis matere.' 240
'It es þe commandement of Criste, þat I ȝow declare,
To kepe it be connande all mankynde clere,
Luke ȝe releue ilke a lede þat lykes ȝoure lare,
To lufe ilk mañ as ȝoure selfe: this lessoñ ȝe lere.' 244
To lere nowe þis ryghte,
Gret Godd of his myghte
Graunte ȝow þe grace! 247
And Ihesu, þat worthi wyghte,
Helpe vs all to þat lyghte
For to see his face! 250

XIV. Saint John. He is taken to Heaven.

(19)

Wyse men͏̃ and witty, þat of thi werkes wyste,
Weled the for wo[r]thi wirchipe to welde ; 252
To be þaire beschope, blithely þay bedde the so blyste,
For þou myghte, in thaire bale, beste be thaire belde;
Thay menskede the with manhede, with mytir vn-myste,
And folowed thi fare freely in frythe and in felde. 256
Thus thow lyffede in the lande whils oure Lorde lyste,
And when͏̃ hym lykede, he laghte the, thi gaste þou gun͏̃
    hym ȝelde.
        For to ȝelde the thi mede,
        In heuen͏̃ for thi gude dede,
            When͏̃ þou heþen͏̃ paste, 261
        He was redy, we rede.
        To þat lyghte he vs lede,
            Þat euer-more salt laste! Amen! 264
            Explicit.

Side notes: The wise men of Ephesus desired St. John to be [leaf 233 bk.] their bishop. — In God's own time, He took St. John to Heaven. — May He light us there too!

[Follows, the prose treatise that begins, 'Praying [MS. Prayng] is a gracyous gyfte of owre lorde godd,' &c.]

XV. EARTH UPON EARTH.

[In a later hand, on leaf 279.]
Memento, Homo, Quod Cinis Es, Et in cinerem Reuerteris[1].
(Five verses of 4: *a a a a*.)

(1)

Limus.
Man of earth
or clay.

Homo primus.

Erthe owte of erthe es wondirly wroghte;
Erthe hase getyn one erthe a dignyte of noghte;
Erthe appon erthe hase sett alle his thoghte,
How þat erthe appon erthe may be heghe broghte. 4

(2)

Sordens.

[lf. 279 bk.]

Erthe appon erthe wolde be a kynge;
Bot howe þat erthe to erthe sall, thynkis he no thynge.
When erthe bredis erthe, and his rentis home brynge[2],
Thane schalle erthe of erthe hafe full harde partynge. 8

(3)

Mutare nequimus.
gets castles
and property,
and says they
are his, and
Vnde

Erthe appon erthe wynnys castells and towrrys;
Thus saise erthe vn-to erthe, 'this es alle owrris;'
When erthe appon erthe hase bigged vp his bowrris,
Than schalle erthe for erthe suffire scharpe stowrrys. 12

(4)

Superbimus.
goes glittering
like gold.

Terram
But he must

Erthe gose appon erthe, as golde appon golde;
He that gose appon erthe gleterande as golde,
Lyke als erthe neuer-more goo to erthe scholde,
And ȝitt schall erthe vn-to erthe ȝa rathere þan he wolde. 16

(5)

turn to earth
again; and
send out
Terra

Redimus.
a foul stink.

Now why þat erthe luffis erthe, wondire me thynke,
Or why þat erthe for erthe scholde oþer swete or swynke
For when þat erthe appon erthe es broghte with-in brynnke;
Thane schalle erthe of erthe hafe a foulle stynke. 20

Mors Soluit Omnia.

[1.] Against the title in the margin is written:—'Perce mihi domine nichil enim sunt dies mei: quid est homo . . . .'
[2] This line is repeated on the leaf's back, with *rentys* for *rentis*.

XVI. SERVE AND LOVE CHRIST.

Robert Thornton's MS. (cir. 1440).

(Twenty alternates: *ab ab*. *Two lines written as one.*)

(1)

Þi Ioy be, ilke a dele,   [leaf 222.]
   To *ser*ue thi Godd' to paye,   Rejoice in
For all this worldes wele   serving God.
   Þou sese it wytes a-waye.   4
Thow fande, his lufe to fele   Try to feel
   Þat laste will w*ith* the aye,   His love.
And þan þi care sall kele
   And pyne t*ur*ne the to playe,   8

(2)

In Criste þou caste thi thoghte,   Hate wrath
   Hate all wrethe and pryde,   and pride.
And thynke þat he þe boghte
   With woundis depe and wyde   12
Whe*n* þou selfe hase soghte,
   Full wele the sall be-tyde;
Of reches, rekke þou noghte   Care not
   Fra helle þat he the hyde.   16 for riches.

(3)

Thay t*ur*ne þaire day to nyghte
   Þat lufes þis erthely sy*n*,
And slayne ere in þat fyghte
   Þare we oure lyfe sall wy*n*.   20
For þat þay lufe vnryghte   Lovers of
   And þare-of kane noghte bly*n*; wrong shall
Þay lose þe lande of lyghte   sit in Hell.
   And hellë sittis with-in.   24

XVI. Serve and Love Christ.

(4)

Lift up your heart to Christ.

Thou do als I þe rede,
　Lyftande vpe thi herte,
And say till hym was ded,
　Criste! my hele þou Arte!　28

Sin weighs you down.

Syn synkës ay as lede,
　And ferrë falles fra qwerte;
For-þi stabill thi stede;
　Þare smyttynge may noghte smerte.　32

(5)

Love your King, Christ,

Lere to lufe thi kynge,
　Whas lufe euer-more will laste;
Haue hym in thi¹ thynkynge,
　And feste his lufe sa faste,　36
That for nane² erthely thynge
　Na qwayntyse may it caste.
Thi sange [be² his, for t]hi swetynge
　He will be at þe laste.　40

(6)

and seek solace in Him.

In Criste² cunayte thi solace;
　His lufë chaunge thi chere;
With Ioy þou take his grace,
　And syghe to sytt hym̄ nere.　44
Euer sekande his face,
　Þou make þi saulë clere³;
He ordaynes hye thi place,
　If þou þis lyfe will lere.　48

(7)

Keep His Ten Commandments,

Thou kepe his byddynges ten̄;
　Halde the fra dedly syn̄;
Forsake þe Ioy of men̄,
　Þat þou his lufe may wyn̄.　52

---

¹ MS. 'in thi thy thynkynge.'　² MS. rubbed.
³ *may* crossed out before *make* in MS.

XVI. *Serve and Love Christ.*

Thi herte, of hym̄ saꝉ bryn̄;
ȝour lufe saꝉ neuer twyn̄;
Langynge he wiꝉ þe len̄,
To won̄ heuen̄ with-in.   *He will make you long for Heaven.* 56

(8)

Thow thynke of his mekenes
  How pure þat he was borne;
Be-halde his bludy flesche
  His heide pungede with thorne.   *Behold His head pierced with thorns,* 60
Þi lufe, þat it noghte lesse,
  He sauede þe, for-lorne,
To serue hym in swetnes
  For aꝉ þat hafe we sworne.   64

(9)

Festyn̄ þi herte to flee   *Flee from this world's cares.*
  Aꝉ þis werldes care,
That þou in ryste may be
  Þou salfe þi saulës sare.   68
His lufe, take it to þe   *Take Christ's love to you,*
  And lufe hym mare & mare,
His face þat þou may see
  When þou saꝉ heþen̄ fare.   72

(10)

If þou be in fandynge,
  Of lufe þou has grete nede,   *which you so need.*
To stedde þe in stabillynge
  And gyffe þe grace to spede.   76
Thow dueꝉ ay with þi kynge,   *Feed ever in Christ's love.*
  And in his lufe þe fede,
For littiꝉ I hafe cunnynge
  To teꝉ of his fairhede.   80

XVI. *Serve and Love Christ.*

(11)

¶ Bot lufe hym at thi myghte
    Whills þou ert lyfande here,
And luke vpe to þat syghte
    Þat moñ be the so dere.   84
Say till hym̄ day and nyghte,
    'Wheñ may I neghe þe nere?
Rayse me vpe to þe, ryghte,
    Thi melodye to here.'   88

(12)

In that lyfe þe stedde,
    Þat þou be ay lufande,
And gyffe hym lufe to wedde,
    Þat þou *with* hym will stande.   92
Ioy in thi breste es bredde
    Wheñ þou erte hym lufande;
Thi saule þan hase he fedde,
    In swete lufe ay brennande.   96

(13)

¶ All vanytese for-sake,
    If þou his lufe will fele;
Thi herte þou hym by-take;
    He cane it kepe full wele.   100
Thi myrthe na mañ may make
    Of Godd' es ilke a dele.
Thi thoghte, late it noghte qwake;
    Thi lufe, late it noghte kele.   104

(14)

¶ Of syñ, þe bitternes,
    Thow flee ay faste þare fraa;
This werldes wikkednes,
    Luke it noghte with þe gaa.   108

XVI. *Serve and Love Christ.* 111

This erthely besynes,
    þat hase men wirkede waa;
Thi lufe it will make lesse,
    If þou it to þe taa.   112

(15)

¶ All we lufe som thynge,
    þat knawynge hase of skyll,
And hafe þare in lykynge,
    When it may com vs till.   116
For-thi, doo Cristes byddynge,
    And lufe hym als he will,
Whas lufe hase nane endynge,
    And Ioye with-owten ill.   120

(16)

¶ Thay þat lufes fleschly,
    Ere lykenede to þe swyne:
In filthe þan will þay lye,
    Thaire fairehede will þay tyne.   124
Thair lufe partes purely
    And puttede es in pyne;
Swetter es lufe gastely,
    þat neuer-mare wyll d[yme].   128

(17)

¶ If þou lufe whils þou may,
    The kynge of mageste,
Thi wa wendis a-way.
    Thi hele hyes to þe,   132
Thi nyghte turnes in-to day,
    Thi blysse mon euer be
When þou erte as I say,
    I pray þe thynke one mee.   136

XVI. *Serve and Love Christ.*

(18)

¶ Ouꝛ thoghtes ſaƚƚ we sette,
   To-gedire in heueꞡ to dueƚƚe,
For þare þe gude er mette,
   Þat Christe haldes fra helle.   140
When we oure synns hafe grett,
   Þe tythandes may we telle,
Þat we fra ferre hase fette
   Þe lufe þat maꞡ saƚƚ feƚƚe.   144

(19)

¶ The werlde, caste it by-hynde,
   And say 'Ihesu, my swete,
Faste in thi lufe me bynde,
   And gyffe me grace to grete,   148
To lufe the, turne my kynde,
   And for to lufe the, I hete
That I thi lufe may fynde,
   Þat wiƚƚ my bales wele bete.   152

(20)

¶ With lufe wounde me with-in,
   And to þi lyghte me lede;
Thow make me clene of synꞡ,
   Þat me thare noghte þe drede.   156
As þou, to saue maꞡ-kynꞡ,
   Sufferd þi sydis to blede,
Gyfe me witt to wynꞡ
   The syghte of þe to mede.'   160

(21)

¶ His lufe es [pure] and trewe,
   Who-so hym lufeande ware,
Sen firste þat I it knewe,
   It kepide me fro care.   164

XVI. *Serve and Love Christ.*

I fand it eu*er* new
To lere me Goddes lare,
And now thaie me noghte rewe
Þat I haffe sufferde sare.   168

(22)

¶ In lufe thi harte þou heghe,
And fyghte to felle þe fende;
Thi dayes sall be vndreghe,
   172

Wheñ thi ded neghes neghe,
And thow sall heþeñ wende,
Thow sall hym see with eghe,
And cum to Criste, thi frende.   176

XVII. [WHAT THUNDER SIGNIFIES IN DIFFERENT MONTHS.]

[*Robert Thornton's MS.* (leaf 50).]

No*tandum*, þat by tokyns off þe Element þat falles In þe moneth, a man schall knawe Plenteth and darke By þe monethes.

In January. Thono*ur* In Ieneuere, sygnyfyes, þat seme ȝere, grette wyndys and grette plentye off cornes, and grette batall also.

In February. Thono*ur* In Feuerȝere, sygnyfyes, þat seme ȝere, þat mony men schall deye, and namlye rychys men.

In March. Thono*ur* In Marche, sygnyfyes, þat seme ȝere, grett wyndes, plentethe off cornes, and grette stryff a-manges þe peple.

In April. Thono*ur* In Auerell, sygnyfyes, þat seme ȝere to be Frutfull & mery, And also grette dede off wekkyde men.

In May. Thono*ur* In May, sygnyfyes, that same ȝere, wyckednese of frut; and grette havng*ur* In many place yt tokneysse.

In June. Thono*ur* In Iune, sygnyfyes, þat same ȝere, woddyse þat or wattyr with dent of wynde schall falle; & grette wodnese of woluese & lyons þat ȝere schall be.

In July. Thono*ur* In Iuly, sygnyfyes, þat same ȝere, a gode ȝer; and grete synner schalle spytt.

[leaf 50 bk.] In October. Thono*ur*[1] In octobyr, sygnyfyes, þat same ȝere, grete wyndys & grete skantenesse of cornnys, & lytyll frowytese on trees.

In November. Thono*ur* In nouembyr, sygnyfyes, þat same ȝere, þat all thynges sall be frowtfull & mery, & also plentethe of cornne.

In December. Thono*ur* In Desembyr, sygnyfyes, þat same ȝere, plentethe of cornes, and mekyll whete and pesse, And reste amanges þe peple of þat rewme þ*er* yt falles In.

---

[1] The upper portion of the original f. 50-50 bk. is lost, hence the signification of thunder in August and September is missing.

[Leaf 51 a. Blank.]

XVIII.
[THE LAMENTATION OF A DYING SINNER.]

Lamentacio Peccatoris.

(1)

All crystyn men þat wawke*s* me bye,   [leaf 51 bk.]
Be-hold & see þis dulful seyght!   Let all Chris-
   tians look on
   me!
I beyd nothere to kawl nor to crye,
I am so dampyd, a woful weyght.   4   I am damned.

(2)

Tayk heyd of me, both kyng & kneyt,
& mend yow heyr qwylle*s* ʒe have space;   Mend your
   ways while
Fore qwen ʒe haue lost euer-lastyng leght,   you have
   time!
Fro mercy be gone, ʒe gayt no grace.   8

(3)

Qwen I was ʒowyng, es now er ʒe,
Þan beyd I neuer a fayrere lyfe:
I spent my ʒerys in vanite,   I wasted my
   life, and I
In vane glory & in stryfe.   12

(4)

I had no hape, qwylle*s* I was heyre,
To ryes & me repent;
Now am I broght apon a beyre:
Itt ys to lett, for I am schentt.   16   am ruind.

(5)

Gret othes, to me þa war ful ryfe,   - I swore
I had no grace for to a-mende;
I sparyd neuer noder madyn ne wyfe,   and whored,
& þat hase browght me to þis ende;   20

XVIII. *The Lamentation of a Dying Sinner.*

(6)

<small>stuft, and</small>

In lecheri I led my lyfe:
Qwen I had God & gud at Wyll,
I sclew my self with-out a knyfe;
In glotonye I toyk my fyll.   24

(7)

<small>lazied.</small>

<small>Now it is 'Had I but known my end!'</small>

In sclewyth I lay, & sclepyd styll;
I was desauyd throw a tryst;
þis dredful ded I druwe my tyll,
And all ys tornyd to adywyst.   28

(8)

<small>Rest not in your sin.
¹ This line is repeated in the MS.</small>

'Add I wyst' yt wyll not bee;
I wot I mune neuer more thweyn,
Fore hym þat dyed for ȝow & me,
Ryes, & rest not in ȝowr synn![1]   32

(9)

<small>[leaf 51 bk., col. 2.]</small>

<small>I had no God but money.</small>

¶ Qwen I was lapyd in synnys seyre,
Sore to yow I mayk my mone,
Þer meght me help no gud prayer;
I had no God, bot gud a-lone.   36

(10)

<small>I was as young (?) blithe as a bird.
Now I suffer.</small>

¶ Qwen I was ȝown, & in my flowres,
I was as blythe as byrd on breyr;
Þat garrys me suffer þese scherp schoris,
And by þis bargan wonder deyre.   40

(11)

<small>Woe to them</small>

<small>who will not take warning by me!</small>

¶ Woo to þes, wer-euer þa bee,
That hase þer v inwyttes to wyll,
Þat wyl not now tayk tent to me,
& knawe þe gud byfor þe yll.   44

XVIII. *The Lamentation of a Dying Sinner.*

(12)

¶ Pure, for fawt, ȝe lat not spyłł,
  For & ȝe do, ȝowr ded ys deght;
The lust of ȝowr fleych wyl neuer ful-fyłł;
  By-war in luste; fer not at ȝe lyght.   48

(13)

¶ In deligat metys I had gret delytt,   *I ate and drank:*
  So had I wyne on-to my pay;
Þat garres þes wormes on me to byt,   *now dragons bite me.*
  And euer þer sang ys 'wyllossay!'   52

(14)

¶ I meght not fast, nor I wold not pray;   *I wouldn't pray.*
  I thoyt to a mendyd in my egge[1];   [¹ *age.*]
I draue euer of, fro day to day,
  And now am I lokyk[2] in a kage.   56   ² *locked.*

(15)

¶ The kage, yt be on byrnyng fyere,   *Now I am in the fire*
  Þat I am ordand in to dwełł:
Thys haue þa gyuyn me to my hyere,
  Euer to last in þe panes of hełł.   60   *of Hell,*

(16)

¶ Thus am I feterd with fendys so fełł,   *bound by fiends like beasts in a stall.*
  As qwo bynd besse in-to a stałł:
Þer ys no tong, my woo kan tełł;
  By-war, gud serys, of syche a fałł!   64 *Take warning by me!*

(17)

¶ Gentyłł brother, haue in mynd,   [*leaf 52.*] *Brother, be*
  Hyen qwen þou schałł weynd away;
To þi awyn sałł, be neuer onkynd,   *not unkind to your soul!*
  Remember þat, bothe nyght & day!   68

XVIII. *The Lamentation of a Dying Sinner.*

(18)

¶ Fuíl derly to hym̄ þat ȝe pray,
   To hym þat was don a-pon a tre,
To safe ȝowr sallis on dowymysday.
   Qwen aíl salles, sauyd mon be.   72

Pray Christ to save you

on Doomsday!

(19)

¶ Than may þer, na lernyd men for ȝow mute,
   No iustys, nor no man of lawe,
For, & þᵃ [do], þᵃ be no buyt,
   Þer charter wyíl not preyf worthe a hawe.   76

Then, no man can

help you.

(20)

¶ Thus euery Man, ȝe tayk gud tent,
   Euery Man in hys de-gre!
Me thynk I heyr a horn blowe:
   Aíl crystyn men, be war by me!   80

Christian men, be warned by me

Explicit lamentacio.

XIX.

[*Robert Thornton's MS.*, leaf 176, col. 2.]

A charme for þe tethe werke.

Say þe charme thris, to it be sayd ix tymes,
And ay thris at a charemynge.

---

(1)

I conjoure the, laythely beste, with þat ilke spere   *I conjure you, loathsome beast,*
Þat Longyous in his hande gan bere,
And also with ane hatte of thorne
Þat one my Lordis hede was borne,   4
With alle þe wordis mare & lesse,
With þe Office of þe Messe,   *by the Mass, by Christ, Our Lady, St. Margaret and St. Katherine,*
With my Lorde and his xij postills,
With oure Lady and hir x Maydenys,   8
[With] Saynt Marg[a]rete þe quene,
Saynt Katerin þe haly virgyne,
ix tymes Goddis forbott, þou wikkyde worme,
Þat euer þou make any rystynge;   12
Bot awaye mote þou wende,   *to go away to earth.*
To þe erde and þe stane!   14

(2)

Thre gude breþer are ȝe;   *You are 3 good brothers.*
Gud gatis gange ȝe!
haly thynges, seke ȝe;   *Seek holy things.*
he says 'will ȝe telle me?'   18
he sais 'blissede Lorde, mot ȝe be!
It may neuer getyn be,

XIX. Charm for the Toothache.

  Lorde, bot ȝour willis be.'
Kneel down and swear to me.
  Settis douñ appoñ ȝour knee,   22
  Gretly athe suere ȝe me,
  By Mary modir mylke so fre.   24
   There es no mañ þat euer hase nede,
  Ȝe schall hym charme, & aske no mede;
I, Christ, will tell you the charm.
  And here sall I lere it the:—
  As þe Iewis wondide me,   28
  Þay wende to wonde me fra þe grounde;
  I helyd my selfe, bathe hale & sounde.
Go to the Mount of Olives, get oil of bays, put it thrice round the worm,
  Ga to þe cragge of Olyuete;
  Take oyle de bayes, þat es so swete;   32
  And thris abowte this worme ȝe strayke;
  This bethe þe worme þat schotte noghte,
  Ne kankire noghte, ne falowe noghte,
  And als clere hale fra þe grounde   36
  Als Ihesu dyde with his faire wondis.
  Þe Fadir, & þe Soñ, & þe Haly Gaste.
and bid it not stay, but go to earth.
  And Goddis forbott, þou wikkyde worme,
  Þat euer þou make any ris[t]ynge or any sugorne![1]   40
  Bot awaye mote þou wende,
  To þe erth and þe stane!   42

[1] or any sugorne *interlined*.

GLOSSARY.

A.

a, *adj.* one, 3/18, 20, 16/10.
abowte-gangande,*prp.* surrounding, 49/6.
adywyst, *sb.* had-I-known (how it would have turned out), after-regret, 116/28; add I wyst, 116/29.
affy, *vb. inf.* trust, 103/214.
agaynestande, *vb. inf.* withstand, 18/21.
aghte, *vb.* 3 *sg. pr.* ought, 64/30, 74/400.
alegeance, *sb.* alleviation, relief, 9/5, 29/29.
alkyn, *adj.* all kinds of, all, 5/14, 7/30, 8/25.
als-swa, *adv.* also, 7/15.
al-per-fyrste, *adv.* first of all, 42/10.
alpire-beste, *adj.* best of all, 32/36.
al-pir-firste, *adj.* first of all, 54/24.
al-pir-myghtyeste, *adj.* mightiest of all, 32/36.
alpirwyseste, *adj.* wisest of all, 32/36.
ambynowre, *sb.* almoner, 56/34.
anehede, *sb.* unity, 47/20, 21, 63/8.
anence, *prep.* anent, concerning, 3/4, 5/11.
anlypy, *adj.* single, 14/14.
anouren, *vb.* 3 *pl. pr.* honour, 23/13.
anoye, *sb.* annoyance, 13/30.
anykyn, *adj.* any kind of, 33/6.
aperte, *adv.* openly, 24/21; in apperte, 23/33; apertely, 47/28; appertly, 40/11.
appropirde, *vb. pp.* attributed, 21/28, 28/32, 33, 34; 48/5.
are, *adv.* before, 7/31.
arely, *adv.* early, 13/7, 60/16.
assethe, *sb.* satisfaction, 7/1.
assoylede, *vb. pp.* absolved, 6/36.
aste, *vb.* 3 *sg. pt.* asked, 98/35.
at, *conj.* that, 31/35, 32/10; *rel. pron.* which, 13/23, 24, 18/12, 13.
at, *prep.* to, 8/29, 26/22, 36/34.
athes, *sb. pl.* oaths, 7/3.

aughte, *sb.* property, possessions, 89/49.
aughten, *adj.* eighth, 6/18, 67/153
aughtened, 29/20.
autyr, *sb.* alter, 8/26.
auauntez, *vb.* 3 *sg. pr.* boasts, vaunts, 24/12.
auauntynge, *sb.* vaunting, 12/18.
avowtry, *sb.* adultery, 14/17.
avysede, *adj.* devised, contrived, 21/9.
awe, *vb.* 3 *sg. pr.* ought, 3/26, 5/10, 8/28; 3 *pl. pr.* 2/1.
awen, *adj.* own, 1/8, 5/1.
ayere, *sb.* air, 1/7.
ayers, *sb. pl.* hairs, 32/30.
aysell, *sb.* vinegar, 70/252.

B.

barett, *sb.* sorrow, pain, 100/117.
barne-tyme, *sb.* brood of children, 61/15.
bathere, *adj.* of both, 9/15.
bawndon, *sb.* control, power, 76/27.
baylyes, *sb. pl.* bailiffs, 55/14.
bayne, *adj.* prompt, ready, 100/97.
bed, *vb.* 3 *pl. pt.* offered, 70/250.
bedde, *vb.* 3 *pl. pt.* beseeched, 105/253.
bede, *sb.* prayer, 77/14.
bedyn, *vb. pp.* bidden, 3/2.
bekende, *vb.* 3 *sg. pt.* consigned, 100/96.
belde, *sb.* comfort, strength, 105/254.
bemes, *sb. pl.* trumpets, 89/37.
benyson, *sb.* blessing, 31/21.
bese, *vb.* 3 *sg. pr.* is, 91/94, 99/73.
besse, *sb. pl.* beasts, 117/62.
besy, *adj.* anxious, careful, 17/16.
besynes, *sb.* trouble, 38/19.
betakynde, *vb. pp.* betokened, 38/18.
bete, *vb. imp.* remedy, 81/71; *inf.* 112/152.
beteche, *vb.* 1 *sg. pr.* commend, 77/10.
bethe, *vb.* 3 *sg. subj.* foments, 120/34.
beyd, *vb.* 1 *sg. pr.* desire, crave, 115/3; 1 *sg. pt.* 115/10.

Glossary

bigged, *vb. pp.* built, 106/11.
birdyn, *sb.* burden, child, 99/71.
bla, *adj.* livid, 94/58.
ble, *sb.* complexion, colour, 91/87; blee, 94/59.
blyn, *vb. inf.* cease, 74/415; blynnes, 3 *sg. pr.* 2/3, 10/30.
blyschede, *pp. adj.* worthy to be blessed, 41/31.
bodyly, *adv.* in the body, 4/12.
bollenynge, *sb.* swelling, 12/32.
bot if, *conj.* unless, 6/36, 8/31.
boustoure, *sb.* ruffian, tyrant, 100/117.
bouxome, *adj.* obedient, 6/2, 54/36
bouxomnes, *sb.* obedience, 54/30.
bown, *adj.* ready, prepared, 70/253, 90/65.
brace, *vb. inf.* embrace, 91/92.
braste, *vb.* 3 *sg. pt.* burst, 44/23.
brede, *vb. pp.* bred, 14/8.
brennande, *vb. prp.* burning, 110/96.
bristez, *vb.* 3 *sg. pr.* bursts, 71/294.
brwke, *vb.* 1 *pl. pr.* enjoy the use of, profit by, 90/80.
brynnynge, *sb.* burning, 23/31.
bryste, *vb. inf.* burst, 59/25.
bufettes, *sb. pl.* blows, 68/202; bofetes, 42/36.
bun, *adj.* 99/71, *v.* bown.
burde, *vb.* 3 *sg. pt.* fell to, behoved, 94/64, 66.
buse, *vb.* 3 *sg. pr.* behoves, 89/38; bude, 3 *sg. pt.* 93/41.
bute, *sb.* remedy, 95/97; buyt, 118/75.
by, *vb. inf.* buy, redeem, 29/12, 36/3.
by-dene, *adv.* at once, 98/48.
by houely, *adj.* helpful, needful, 5/21.
by-leue, *sb.* belief, 52/29, 30.
byrde, *sb.* woman, lady, maiden, 97/7, 99/71.
byse, *sb.* sort of fine stuff, 67/147.

C.

carpyng, *sb.* uttering, speaking, 7/35.
cayre, *vb. inf.* go, 98/46.
caytefly, *adv.* wretchedly, 40/19.
caytifede, *adj.* made captive, wretched, 38/28.
chasty, *vb. inf.* chastise, correct, 10/1, 22/26; chastied, *pp.* 22/25.
chaufe, *vb.* 3 *sg. pr.* make warm, 81/53.
chese, *vb. inf.* choose, 11/20, 29/36.
clergy, *sb.* clergydom, 103/210.

clethe, *vb. inf.* clothe, 9/27, 22/20; clede, 3 *pl. pt.* 69/222.
collacyone, *sb.* discourse, 23/26.
comforthe, *sb.* comfort, 55/20.
comfurthe, *vb. inf.* comfort, 55/2.
communers, *sb.* partakers, 1/11.
comonynge, *sb.* communion, 3/22.
comouns, *vb.* 3 *pl. pr.* commune, 3/24.
complyn, *sb.* last service of the day, 45/29.
conabilly, *adv.* suitably, 19/13.
conande, *adj.* cunning, skilful, 51/13.
conandely, *adv.* thoroughly, 14/33; cunnandely, 14/35.
conaundenes, *sb.* skill, wisdom, knowledge, 13/21.
conclude, *vb. inf.* confute, 90/67.
contekes, *sb. pl.* contests, 25/4.
contende, *vb. pp.* contained, 31/29, 38/12.
cop(p)e, *sb.* cup, 34/29, 30.
couaite, *vb. inf.* covet, desire, 27/36, 28/6; couayte, 1 *sg. pr.* 80/41; coueites, 3 *sg. pr.* 14/32; couaytes, 3 *pl. pr.* 27/22.
couetyse, *sb.* covetousness, 6/26.
cufere, *vb. inf.* cover, 90/77.
cun, *vb. inf.* know, 2/35, 14/27; 1 *pl. pr.* 10/6; 3 *pl. pr.* 2/28, 33; cunnes, 3 *pl. pr.* 14/31.
cunnynge, *sb.* knowledge, wisdom, experience, 24/27, 28/22, 29.

D.

dalfe, *vb.* 3 *sg. pt.* delved, 88/1.
darke = darthe, *sb.* dearth, scarcity, 114/2.
daynte, *adj.* precious, excellent, handsome, 97/17.
debonerte, *sb.* gentleness, mildness, 86/92.
dede, *sb.* death, 3/27, 4/22, 9/5, 27/18, &c.
dedeyned, *vb. pp.* displeased, 100/111.
defaste, *vb. pp.* defaced, 99/67.
defaute, *sb.* fault, want, 2/8, 28/30.
defendis, *vb.* 3 *sg. pr.* forbids, 29/26; defendyde, *pp.* 24/9, 26/30.
defule, *vb. inf.* trample under foot, spurn, 48/26.
delfynge, *sb.* burying, 102/154.
deligat, *adj.* delicate, 117/49.
demynge, *sb.* judging, 61/17.
dent, *sb.* blowing, 114/15.

Glossary. 123

dere, *adj.* dear, 94/64.
dere, *sb.* injury, 101/126.
derfe, *adj.* hard, brutal, 101/125.
dessayues, *vb.* 3 *sg. pr.* deceives, 25/26; dessayfede, *pp.* 18/14.
dill, *adj.* foolish, stupid, 101/125.
dispendis, *vb.* 3 *pl. pr.* spend, 31/17.
doghtyrs, *sb. pl.* daughters, 61/13.
doluen, *pp.* buried, 4/17.
domme, *adj.* dumb, 58/18.
dortoure, *sb.* dormitory, 53/15.
doungen, *vb. pp.* beaten, struck, 43/11.
dowte, *vb. inf.* fear, 23/28.
doynge owte, *sb.* turning out, 8/30.
dredles, *adv.* doubtlessly, 102/154.
drery, *adj.* sad, 85/52.
dreryly, *adv.* miserably, 32/29.
drewrye, *sb.* love, 81/65.
drowry, *sb.* gift, precious thing, 97/17.
druwe, *vb.* 1 *sg. pt.* drew, 116/27.
duellyde, *vb. pp.* remained, 18/35.
dule, *sb.* pain, suffering, grief, sorrow, 73/359, 100/112.
dule, *adj.* foolish, erring, 97/18.
dulful, *adj.* doleful, 115/2.
duse, *vb.* 3 *sg. pr.* does, 29/20; 3 *pl. pr.* 10/8, 13/6, 14/17.
dyme, *vb. inf.* grow dim, 111/128.
dynge, *adj.* worthy, 65/93.
dyspende, *vb.* 1 *pl. pr.* destroy, 23/5; *pp.* dissipated, 17/30.
dyssayued, *vb. pp.* deceived, 37/1.
dysses, *sb.* trouble, 26/7.
dyssessede, *vb. pp.* disseized, dispossessed, 7/5.

E.

efter, *prep.* according to, 5/27, 7/27, 9/10; eftere, 6/4; eftyre, 22/16.
eghe, *sb.* eye, 16/24, 35/24; eghne, *pl.* 53/11.
eke, *vb. inf.* increase, 73/348; ekes, 3 *pl. pr.* 54/18.
elde, *sb.* age, 2/30, 7/27, 8/28, &c.
encheson, *sb.* cause, occasion, 16/13, 27/19, 94/68.
endent, *vb. pp.* fixed in, inlaid, 97/17.
endeynede,*vb.*3 *sg. pt.* condescended, deigned, 97/18.
enflawmes, *vb.* 3 *sg. pr.* inflames, 59/22.
er(e), *vb.* are, 3 *pl. pr.* 2/21, 5/10, 7/10, 30; erte, 2 *sg. pr.* 17/21.

euen, *adj.* equal, 3/13, 15; euynne, 4/30.
evencristen, *sb.* fellow-Christian, 5/12, 11/6, 12/22, 24/32, &c.
evenhede, *sb.* moderation, 11/29.

F.

faamen, *sb. pl.* foemen, enemies, 84/50, 101/128.
faas, *sb. pl.* foes, 11/25.
faere, *adj. cp.* fewer, 47/16.
falachipe, *sb.* fellowship, 19/23.
fallace, *sb.* deceitfulness, 90/77.
falles, *vb.* 3 *pl. pr.* belong, 2/20, 3/5, 6.
falowe, *vb.* 3 *sg. pr.* fades, 120/35.
fande, *vb. inf.* endeavour, try, tempt, 18/21; *imper.* 12/12, 107/5; fandes, 1 *pl. pr.* 6/7.
fandynge, *sb.* temptation, 11/26, 21/8.
fange, *vb.* 3 *sg. pt.* took, 93/45.
fawt, *sb.* fault, 117/45.
feblesce, *sb.* feebleness, 40/34.
feele, *adj.* many, 101/145.
felaschepe, *sb.* fellowship, 47/12, 13.
felawrede, *sb.* fellowship, 8/23.
fellenes, *sb.* terror, awfulness, 48/7.
fere, *adj.* able to go, strong, healthy, 88/11; ferre, 108/30.
fere, *sb.* companion, wife, mate, 99/60, 104/238.
*ferly, *sb.* wonder, miracle, 99/86.
fermoresse, *sb.* hospital nurse, 57/24.
fermory(e), *sb.* hospital, infirmary, 53/23, 57/25.
fet, *vb.* 3 *sg. pt.* fetched, brought, 98/31; fette, *pp.* 112/143.
feule,*sb.* bird, 14/7; fewle, 88/12.
filede, *vb. pp.* fouled, defiled, 99/59.
flemede, *vb.* 3 *pl. pt.* put to flight, 101/128.
flesche-foldes, *sb. pl.* flesh, 90/56.
flom, *sb.* river, 68/175.
flytynge, *sb.* quarrelling, 13/1.
foghles, *sb. pl.* birds, 65/80.
foly, *vb. inf.* fool, 6/10.
fone, *adj.* few, 31/17, 99/86.
forbeddes, *vb.* 3 *sg. pr.* forbids, 6/10.
forboden, *vb. pp.* forbidden, 5/14, 6/20.
forbott, *sb.* prohibition, 119/11.
forbysen, *sb.* example, 78/361.
force, *sb.* necessity, 47/3.
for-do, *vb. inf.* destroy, 13/2.
forhewe,*vb. inf.* avoid, forsake, 12/4.

124 Glossary.

forluke, sb. foresight, providence, 4/20.
forme-fadyrs, sb. forefathers, 1/17, 21, 4/20.
for-thi, conj. therefore, 2/11, 28/29.
for-thi þat, conj. because, in order that, 2/4, 35, 14/15.
forthynkynge, sb. repentance, 8/18.
for-why, conj. because, 55/5.
founde, vb. inf. go, hasten, 85/70, 79.
fourtede, adj. fourth, 4/27.
fratour, sb. refreshment-room of monastery, refectory, 53/14, 56/27.
frayste, vb. inf. try, test, experience, learn, ask, 99/73, 101/146, 104/226, 237.
frele, adj. frail, 18/21.
frely, adj. free, noble, courteous, 99/74, 85.
fremmede, adj. not of kin, foreign, 6/11, 61/7.
frenes, sb. freedom, liberty, 40/34.
frowytese, sb. pl. fruits, 114/20.
frythe, sb. forest, 105/256.
fude, sb. offspring, person, 89/27, 93/23, 98/31, 99/74.
fule, sb. fool, 69/207.
ful(l)e, adj. foul, evil, 11/26, 30, 42/34.
fulle, vb. inf. foul, defile, 42/34.
fyaunce, sb. trust, 86/89.
fychede, vb. 3 pl. pt. fixed, 70/242.
fyle, vb. inf. defile, 68/182; **fylede,** pp. 93/28.

G.

gapaunde, vb. prp. gaping, 70/246.
garnere, sb. granary, 58/1.
garrys, vb. 3 sg. pr. makes, 116/39.
gase, vb. 3 sg. pr. goes, 90/54.
gastely, adj. spiritual, 10/28.
gate, vb. 3 sg. pt. begot, 75/11.
gates, sb. pl. roads, ways, 101/144, 119/16.
gayne, adj. convenient, 101/144.
gayt, vb. 2 pl. pr. get, 115/8.
gedyre, vb. inf. gather, include, 35/9; **gedire,** sg. imper. 48/18; **gedyrde,** pp. 48/19; **gedirde,** 32/12.
gelery, sb. deceit, trickery, 13/20.
gelouse, adj. jealous, 58/22.
gente, adj. noble, 97/15.
gere, vb. 3 sg. pr. causes, 13/8; **gerte,** pp. 7/4.
germandir, sb. (?) some precious stone, 97/15.
gerne, adv. eagerly, 101/143.
gernere, sb. garner, 53/24.

geste, sb. guest, 91/91.
gete, sb. jet, 97/15.
getes, vb. 3 pl. pr. beget, 5/33; **getyn,** pp. 4/9; **get,** 98/29.
gome, sb. man, 98/29.
gouernaylle, sb. ruler, 35/10.
grauen, vb. pp. buried, 29/12.
graythely, adj. well-formed, excellent, worthy, 98/29.
graythely, adv. quickly, readily, 101/144.
grete, vb. inf. cry, 103/187; **grett,** 3 pl. pt. 103/187.
greuosere, adj. cp. more grievous, more harmful, 14/18.
grewe, sb. Greek, 47/8.
gruche, vb. 2 sg. imp. grudge, 49/36.
grysse, sb. grass, 22/5.
gulyardy, sb. buffoonery, ribaldry, 37/6.
gun, vb. 3 sg. pt. began, 71/276, 92/20; 2 sg. pt. 72/336.
gysed, vb. 2 sg. pt. didst prepare, 101/143

H.

habyde, vb. inf. abide, wait for, 89/47; **habade,** 3 sg. pt. 19/22.
hailsed, vb. 3 pl. pt. hailed, 101/149.
haldande, sb. pl. holders, possessors, 31/8.
halden, vb. pp. bound (under obligation), 38/13.
hale, adj. whole, sound, 8/26.
hally, adj. holy, 1/20, 27.
haloghes, sb. saints, 77/17; **halous,** 21/7; **halowes,** 5/28.
hape, sb. (good) fortune, 115/13.
hase, vb. 3 sg. pr. has, 1/21, 3/27; 3 pl. pr. 1/20, 2/8, 7/25.
hateredyn, sb. hatred, 12/24, 25/21, 41/1.
hatten, vb. pp. called, 12/21.
haunkede, vb. pp. entangled, 12/10.
hauntede, vb. pp. practised, 14/5.
hauynge, sb. possessions, power, 6/9.
hawe, sb. haw (fruit of hawthorn), 90/63, 118/76.
heghe, adj. high, 3/11.
heghenees, sb. haughtiness, 12/15.
heghyng, sb. exaltation, 24/6.
heide, sb. head, 109/60.
heldes, vb. 3 sg. pr. inclines, 25/18; **helde,** 3 sg. pt. 44/21.
hele, sb. health, salvation, 3/25, 5/34, 9/6.
hele, vb. inf. conceal, 46/7; **helede,** 3 sg. pt. 46/12.

Glossary. 125

heledide, vb. 3 pl. pt. submitted, 104/230.
helelynge, sb concealing, 6/17.
helere, sb. healer, saviour, 67/140.
hende, adj. gracious, 99/80; hendeste, super. 104/229.
hendely, adv. graciously, 57/11.
herber(e), vb. inf. harbour, shelter, 9/28, 30/13.
herbery, sb. harbour, refuge, 30/19.
herere, sb. hearer, 12/30.
herne-panne, sb. skull, 69/226.
heryede, vb. 3 sg. pt. harried, 4/19.
hete, vb. 1 sg. pr. tell, promise, 89/50.
hete, vb. 1 sg. pr. grow hot, 112/150.
hethyng(e), sb. scorn, contempt, ridicule, 40/25, 42/33, 68/200.
hepen, adv. hence, 9/7, 105/261.
heuede, sb. head, power, 5/34; adj. chief, 12/2, 8.
heuenes, sb. heaviness, 14/2.
hey, adj. high, 4/30.
heyn, adv. hence, 85/70.
hide, vb. pp. hidden, 59/20.
highte, vb. 3 sg. pt. was called, 61/15, 16.
hippynge, sb. jumping over or omitting part of the service, 40/26.
homerynge, sb. muttering, 40/26.
horssyng, sb. equipage, 24/30.
howgates, adv. in what manner, how, 27/2.
hyen, adv. hence, 117/66.
hyghte, vb. 2 sg. pt. promised, 26/26; hyghttes, 3 sg. pt. 59/15.
hyne, sb. pl. servants, 104/230.
hynge, vb. inf. hang, 100/92.

I.

in-gate, sb. entrance, 53/9, 57/3.
inmanges, prep. among, 48/1.
inspayre, sb. breathing, breath, 75/7.
intill, prep. into, 10/33.
inwyttes, sb. pl. senses, 116/42.

iage, sb. jerk, 70/243.

K.

kan, vb. 2 sg. pr. knowest, 19/35.
kawl, vb. inf. call, 115/3.
kele, vb. inf. cool, 107/7; 3 sg. pr. 19/29.
kenn, vb. inf. teach, make known, 35/8; kennes, 3 sg. pr. 11/18, 16/20; kennde, 3 sg. pt. 31/30; kende, pp. 14/23, 22/31.

kennynge, sb. instruction, 22/24.
kide, vb. 2 sg. pt. didst show, 66/101.
knaue, sb. servant, 6/31, 102/168.
knaweliggynge, sb. knowledge, 59/19.
konn, vb. 3 sg. pr. knows, 29/36.
kychynnere, sb. cook, 56/20.
kye, sb. pl. cows, 22/20.
kynd(e), sb. nature, 3/28, 4/29, 32, 12/16.
kyndely, adv. by nature, 14/7, 8.
kynredyn, sb. kindred, 18/29.

L.

lache, vb. inf. seize, 13/32; laghte, 3 sg. pt. 105/258.
laddes, sb. pl. lads, men, 100/116.
lame, sb. loam, 88/5.
lange, vb. inf. long, 93/41.
langes, vb. 3 pl. pr. belongs, 1/27; langande, prp. 30/16.
large, adj. liberal, generous, 49/10, 13, 75/421.
latesommes, sb. tardiness, backwardness, 13/32.
lattly, adv. late, 18/13.
lawe, adj. low, 38/19.
lawede, adj. unlearned, lay, 5/26.
lawede, vb. 3 sg. pt. lowered, humbled, 34/7.
layke, sb. sport, amusement, 40/25.
laytheste, adj. most hateful, 100/115.
ledden, vb. 3 pl. pt. led, 100/116.
lede, sb. man, person, people, land, 97/20, 100/115, 103/211, 104/243.
lefe, vb. inf. leave, abandon, 35/30.
leffe, vb. 1 sg. pr. believe, trust, 74/410.
lefte, vb. 3 sg. pr. lift, 48/20.
lefulle, adv. permissible, lawful, 8/4.
lele, adj. faithful, 32/26.
lelly, adv. faithfully, 26/24, 95/87.
len, vb. inf. give, lend, 109/55; lennes, 2 sg. pr. 77/5.
lende, vb. inf. remain, reside, tarry, 98/47, 99/78, 103/211; 3 sg. pr. 80/47.
lere, vb. inf. teach, learn, 2/10, 30; leres, 3 sg. pr. 26/8; lere, 3 pl. pr. 2/27; lerede, pp. 2/5.
lerede, adj. learned, 5/26, 8/7.
leryng, sb. learning, 1/26.
les(s)e, vb. inf. loose, 6/22, 7/4.
lesses, vb. 3 sg. pr. lessens, 24/16.
lessynge, sb. lessening, 9/7.
lesynge, sb. lying, 92/4; pl. lies, 6/21.

126 Glossary.

lete by, vb. 3 sg. pt. esteem, value, 97/20; lett, 3 pl. pt. 103/192.
lettes, vb. 3 sg. pr. hinders, 11/30, 14/3, 78/3; lettis, 3 pl. pr. 26/4.
leue, sb. belief, 14/16.
leue, vb. 1 pl. pr. believe, 5/13.
leue, adj. dear, beloved, 54/19.
lewde, adj. unlearned, lay, 8/7.
lewte, sb. loyalty, 57/24.
lodde, sb. people, men, 90/55.
lofe, vb. inf. praise, glorify, 34/1; louede, pp. 33/9.
loos, sb. praise, 24/28.
lorne, vb. pp. lost, 67/141.
losengery, sb. flattery, 26/6.
lowssynge, sb. loosing, setting free, 9/16.
lowte, vb. 1 pl. pr. bow, worship, 5/13.
lufe-frayners, sb. pl. love-seekers, 62/7.
lugede, vb. pp. lodged, 97/5.
lurdans, sb. pl. lazy persons, rascals, 100/115.
lyfelade, sb. livelihood, 6/8.
lygge, vb. inf. lie, 59/28.
lyghte, adj. easy, 18/21.
lyghtenes, sb. alleviation, ease, 9/5, 40/33, 41/6.
lyghtly, adv. easily, 14/6.
lyghtnes, vb. 3 sg. pr. enlightens, 59/19.
lykande, adj. pleasing, 12/15.
lykede, vb. 3 sg. pt. pleased, 92/16.
lyknes, sb. comparison, 24/18.
lykynge, sb. pleasure, 5/29, 11/30.
lyne, sb. linen, 22/20.
lyte, sb. tardiness, 13/32.
lythe, sb. people, men, tenants, 6/26, 7/5; lythes, 98/48.

M.

male-eese, sb. distress, discomfort, 19/31.
malese, sb. malice, 61/18.
mane, sb. complaint, 80/29.
mase, vb. 3 sg. pr. makes, 17/10; 3 pl. pr. 58/25.
maun, vb. 1 pl. pr. must, 8/23:
mawmetis, sb. pl. idols, 103/216.
mawmetryes, sb. idolatries, 5/15.
mayne, sb. power, 91/87, 101/140.
maystry, sb. mastery, dominion, 103/216.
medles, adj. profitless, 40/26.
mekill, adj. & adv. much, many, 1/19, 20, 2/4.

mekillnes, sb. greatness, 80/32.
mekyde, vb. pp. humbled, made meek, 22/30.
mele, vb. inf. speak, 103/186.
mene, vb. inf. moan, communicate, tell, 98/28, 44; 1 sg. pr. 85/51.
menesyng, sb. mention, 98/34.
mengede, vb. pp. mixed, 5/3.
menskede, vb. 3 pl. pt. honoured, 105/255.
menȝe, sb. household, 24/30, 104/234.
merrede, vb. 3 sg. pt. hindered, 103/215.
merres, vb. 3 sg. pr. hinders, 88/4.
merryng, sb. marring, impairment, 4/6.
mesure, sb. moderation, 28/13.
mete, adj. fit, meet, 4/30.
methe, adj. modest, 99/57.
methe, or methefulness, sb. temperance, 11/28.
mett, sb. measure, 11/32.
mobles, sb. pl. movable goods, 98/43.
moghte, vb. 3 sg. pr. might, 18/1, 6.
momellynge, sb. mumbling, 40/26.
mon, vb. 3 sg. pr. will, 89/41; 1 pl. pr. 90/75; 2 pl. pr. 54/11.
mone, vb. sg. imp. communicate, tell, 104/239.
mortasse, sb. mortise, 70/242.
mot, vb. 3 sg. pr. must, 62/14.
mouande, vb. prp. moving, 64/43.
mukke, sb. muck, 17/21.
munne, vb. 1 sg. pr. shall, 116/30.
mute, vb. inf. plead, 118/73.
mynynge, sb. lessening, 4/6.
mysdose, vb. 3 pl. pr. do amiss, 10/4.
mysese, sb. distress, misery, 30/23.
myster, sb. need, 9/31, 25/35, 27/9, &c.
mystraste, vb. inf. doubt, 36/8.
mytir, sb. mitre, 105/255.

N.

namely, adv. especially, 2/13.
nate, sb. pl. cattle, 22/19.
neddyrs, sb. pl. adders, 17/24.
nede, adv. of necessity, 47/14, 21.
neese, sb. nose, 17/1; nese, 48/31.
neghe, vb. inf. approach, 110/86.
nesche, vb. inf. soften, 33/11.
neuen, vb. 1 pl. pr. name, 5/22; neuenede, pp. 13/4; nevynn, inf. 17/23.

Glossary. 127

noblaye, *sb.* splendour, grandeur, 12/16.
noresohe, *vb. inf.* nourish, 64/44.
noyande, *adj.* hurtful, 22/22, 65/63.
noye, *vb. inf.* annoy, hurt, 22/29.
noye, *sb.* hurt, injury, 26/6, 88/6.
nyende, *adj.* ninth, 6/24.

O.

o, *prep.* of, from, 90/55.
oftesythe(s), *adv.* often, 2/6, 13/7.
okyr, *sb.* usury, 13/19.
one, *prep.* in, on, 2/16, 3/2, 4/21, &c.
or, *adv.* before, 90/54.
orloge, *sb.* timepiece, 60/16, 17.
ouerhope, *sb.* over-confidence, 11/2.
ouermekill, *adv.* too much, 11/24.
ouer-tane, *vb. pp.* overcome, 58/10.
ouper . . . or, *conj.* either . . . or, -37/30.
owterage, *sb.* excess, 11/29.

P.

parisohennes, *sb.* parishioners, 2/26.
pay(e), *sb.* satisfaction, 107/2,117/50.
pay(e), *vb. inf.* please, satisfy, 10/27, 40/23, 57/20; payes, 3 *pl. pr.* 56/1.
pelars, *sb. pl.* pillars, 52/36.
penetancere, *sb.* one who imposes penance, confessor, 58/32.
perawnter, *adv.* peradventure, 2/8.
pereles, *adj.* peerless, 98/38.
perry, *sb.* precious stones, 97/16.
pertenande, *adj.* pertaining, 28/8.
petance, *sb.* share, provision, 59/13.
pete, *sb.* pity, 20/23.
poleschesy, *sb.* 57/30.
pouste, *sb.* power, 68/168, 98/38.
preste, *adv.* quickly, readily, 91/91.
preue, *adj.* intimate, 99/83.
pungede, *vb. pp.* pricked, 109/60.
pure, *adj.* poor, 11/14, 31/3, 117/45.
puruaye, *vb. inf.* provide, 28/22 ; purvayede, *pp.* provided, 22/15.
purueance, *sb.* providence, 76/19.
pyssmowre, *sb.* ant, 22/33.
pystill, *sb.* epistle, 2/12, 11/8.

Q.

qwaynte, *adj.* skilful, clever, 18/1.
qwayntyse, *sb.* skill, wisdom, 108/38.
qweire, *sb.* choir, 40/14.
qwerte, *sb.* sound health, 108/30.
qwykke, *adj.* living, 3/29, 65/74.
qwylles, *adv.* while, 115/6.

R.

racede, *vb.* 3 *sg. pt.* tore, 69/219.
rathely, *adv.* quickly, 90/64.
raue, *vb.* 3 *pl. pt.* broke, opened, 44/24, 70/245.
raueschea, *vb.* 3 *sg. pr.* ravishes, 56/15 ; raueschede, *pp.* 58/10.
raughte, *vb. pp.* reached, given, 89/49.
rawe, *sb.* row, 89/37.
reall, *adj.* royal; 67/142.
relyede, *vb.* 3 *sg. pt.* rallied, 97/6.
resafe, *vb. inf.* receive, 57/11 ; reschayfe, 27/1 ; rescheyue, 8/28 ; ressayfes, 2 *sg. pr.* 45/28 ; ressayues, 3 *pl.pr.* 7/28; ressayfede, 2 *sg. pt.* 45/28 ; rescheyuede, *pp.* 17/29.
reste, *sb.* arrest, 25/12.
reuer, *sb.* river, 52/5.
reuthe, *sb.* sorrow, sadness, 94/61.
reuyng, *sb.* robbing, 6/16.
rewly, *adv.* sadly, dreadfully, 89/37.
rewme, *sb.* realm, 55/14.
ruggede, *vb.* 3 *sg. pt.* tore, 90/66.
rynnand, *adj.* smooth, fluent, 36/31.
rysesynge, *sb.* rising, 4/26.
ryste, *sb.* rest, peace, 53/6, 55/16, &c.
ryuely, *adv.* frequently, 7/9.

S.

saghe, *vb.* 1 *pl. pt.* saw, 35/23 ; 2 *sg. pt.* 84/40.
salfe, *vb. imp.* salve, 109/68.
samen, *adv.* together, 3/33, 9/15, 10/32 ; samenly, 3/14.
sane, *vb. inf.* heal, 93/40. *Cotgr.* 'Saner. To cure, heal, or make whole.'
sassyng, *sb.* holding, observing, 67/157.
sauoyre, *sb.* pleasure, 59/8, 19.
saynede, *vb.* 2 *sg. pt.* didst bless, 102/173, 104/227, 228.
schede, *vb. inf.* divide, separate, 64/45.
schenchipe, *sb.* ignominy, punishment, 22/16.
schente, *vb.pp.* disgraced, confounded, 84/34.
schere, *vb. inf.* cut, 67/161.
schire, *adj.* pure, 59/11.
scho, *pron.* she, 35/2, 4.
schope, *vb.* 3 *sg. pt.* shaped, created, 75/3.

schoris, *sb. pl.* pangs, pains, 116/39.
schotte, *vb.* 3 *sg. pr.* 120/34.
sckathe, *vb. inf.* injure, 27/33.
segge, *sb.* man, 101/142.
seghes, *vb.* 3 *sg. pr.* sees, 46/26.
sek(e)nes, *sb.* sickness, 4/24, 9/5, 30.
sekerly, *adv.* securely, certainly, 38/13.
sekyr, *adj.* secure, 10/28.
selcouthe, *adj.* strange, wonderful, 100/88.
sely, *adj.* happy, 54/5; cely, 54/17.
sembyll, *vb. inf.* assemble, gather, 57/31.
semle, *sb.* meeting, battle, 101/142.
sen, *conj.* since, 43/26, 46/28.
sere, *adj.* several, particular, 3/18, 12/18,65/62,98/36; *adv.* severally, 65/59.
serues, *vb.* 3 *sq. pr.* deserves, 5/2.
sesede, *vb. pp.* seized, possessed, 72/340.
seyn, *adv.* afterwards, 93/27.
seynge, *sb.* seeing, 16/24.
seys, *vb.* 3 *sg. pr.* sees, 58/11.
skikk ande skekke, *vb. inf.* rob and plunder, 90/59.
skillwyse, *adj.* possessed of reason, reasonable, 1/14, 8/31, 9/4.
skornande, *vb. pp.* mocking, 69/228.
skourgegynge, *sb.* scourging, 69/215.
skowreghide, *vb. pp.* scourged, 69/211.
skyll, *sb.* reason, 1/8, 22/19.
skynm, *sb.* scum, 18/26.
sla(a), *vb. inf.* slay, 27/14, 85/65; 1 *pl. pr.* 6/5; 3 *pl. pr.* 12/9; slaas, 3 *sg. pr.* 12/13; slaes, 27/17; slane, *pp.* 80/31.
slake, *vb. inf.* slacken, 95/105.
slawenes, *sb.* sloth, 13/29.
sleghenes, *sb.* wisdom, sagacity, 11/17.
sleghte, *sb.* wisdom, sagacity, 11/16.
slewthe, *sb.* sloth, 13/29.
slokyns, *vb.* 3 *sg. pr.* extinguishes, 25/8.
slyke, *adj.* such, 56/32, 58/13.
smate, *vb.* 3 *sg. pt.* smote, 43/1.
sonne, *adv.* soon, 35/29.
sothefaste, *adj.* true, 3/11, 8/18; sothefastly, *adv.* 3/13.
sowe, *vb. inf.* grieve, 85/72.
sown, *vb. inf.* sound, 12/24.
sownnes, *vb.* 3 *sg. pr.* sounds, 48/7.
sparre, *vb.* 2 *sg. imp.* bar, close, 53/7.
spensere, *sb.* butler, steward, 56/33.

speres, *vb.* 3 *sg. pr.* bars, fastens, 57/2.
spire, *vb. inf.* inquire, 88/2.
spousebreke, *sb.* adultery, 14/18.
spyll, *vb. inf.* destroy, perish, 72/324, 93/39.
spytt, *for* spyll, *vb. inf.* 114/18.
stabill, *vb. inf.* establish, 55/14; stabylls, 3 *sg. pr.* 58/6.
stalleworthe, *adj.* stalwart, strong, 8/14.
stalworthenes, *sb.* strength, stalwartness, 25/33, 26/11.
stallworthy, *adv.* stalwartly, courageously, 26/9.
stamerynge, *sb.* hesitation, 14/10.
stedde, *vb. inf.* place, 109/75.
stede, *sb.* place, 8/17, 22/14.
steighe, *vb.* 3 *sg. pt.* ascended, 29/15; stey(e), 4/28, 33; stey, 2 *sg. pt.* 73/367.
steke,*vb.* 2.*sg. imp.* shut, close,53/11.
steskys *for* stekys, *vb.* 3 *sg. pr.* fastens, shuts, 53/4.
steuene, *sb.* voice, 79/11.
stowrrys, *sb. pl.* conflicts, pangs, 106/12.
strange, *adj.* strong, 55/6.
strayke, *vb.* 3 *pl. pr.* rub gently, 120/33.
strydand, *prp.* striving, throbbing (with more than usual force), 70/248.
strynde, *sb.* generation, 93/27.
stynte, *vb. inf.* stop, 72/339.
styre, *vb. inf.* move, 67/162.
sudayne, *adj.* sudden, 76/36, 77/20.
suellynge, *sb.* swallowing, 17/1; sweloynge, *sb.* 48/25.
suget, *sb.* subject, 64/41; sugettes, *pl.* church-members, parishioners, 2/27, 31.
suggeourned, *vb.* 2 *sg. pt.* didst sojourn, 101/141.
surquytry, *sb.* presumption, 24/10.
suyle, *sb.* soil, country, 101/141.
swelowe, *vb. inf.* swallow, 70/254; swelawes, 3 *sg. pr.* 48/31.
swetis, *vb.* 3 *sg. pr.* sweats, 56/22.
sybb(e), *adj.* near of kin, related, 6/11, 14/20, 99/69.
syll, *sb.* floor, earth, 103/201.
syment, *sb.* cement, 52/31.
synner, *sb.* (?) error in transcription, 114/18.
synows, *sb. pl.* sinews, 69/236.
syte, *sb.* pain, 12/21.
sythes, *sb. pl.* times, 18/4.

Glossary.

T.

taa, *vb.* 2 *sg. pr.* take, 111/112; tase, 3 *sg. pr.* 8/32, 33; 3 *pl. pr.* 9/9; tane, *pp.* 4/17, 7/34, &c.
tades, *sb. pl.* toads, 17, 24.
taken, *vb. pp.* indicated, 38/14.
tane, *adj.* one, 7/11.
temperoure, *sb.* temper, 25/3.
tente, *vb. inf.* try, 5/29.
thede, *sb.* people, country, 100/113.
thee-banes, *sb. pl.* thigh-bones, 45/2.
thewe, *sb.* virtue, 10/19, 27; *pl.* 52/16, 57/9.
thir, *pron. nom. pl.* these, 4/1.
thole, *vb. inf.* suffer, 70/271; tholede, 2 *sg. pt.* 70/272; 3 *sg. pt.* 4/12, 56/18.
thole-mode, *adj.* patient, 10/3.
thonour, *sb.* thunder, 114/4.
thraly, *adv.* boldly, severely, 100/114.
threhed, *sb.* trinity, 63/7.
threted, *vb.* 3 *pl. pt.* oppressed, 100/114.
thweyn, *vb. inf.* (?) (a word ending in -*in* is wanted, to rhyme with *sin*).
till, *prep.* to, 1/27, 4/2, 9/34, &c.
tite, *adv.* soon, quickly, 20/1.
to-braste, *vb.* 3 *pl. pt.* burst asunder, 69/236.
to-reuen, *vb. pp.* torn, 69/213.
tother, toper, *adj.* other, second, 3/11, 7/12, 11/7.
traiste, *vb. inf.* trust, hope, 10/33, 11/2; traystes, 3 *pl. pr.* 5/17.
trauelde, *vb. pp.* troubled, 18/15.
tray, *sb.* trouble, annoyance, 1/25.
trayste, *sb.* trust, faith, 10/30, 31, 28/17.
traystely, *adv.* trustfully, confidently, 36/15.
trouthe, *sb.* faith, belief, 45/23, 46/10.
trow(e), *vb. inf.* believe, 3/9, 10, 47/4; trowes, 1 *pl. pr.* 45/24; trowande, *prp.* 21/5.
trowyng, *sb.* believing, 38/17.
twesste, *adj.* twelfth, 67/163.
twyn, *adj.* two, 13/17.
twyn, *vb. inf.* separate, 18/3, 21/12; twynnede, *pp.* 33/16.
tyne, *vb. inf.* lose, 111/124; tynes, 2 *sg. pr.* 40/20; tynt(e), *pp.* 17/31, 19/17, 66/128.
tyte, *adv.* soon, quickly, 23/26, 32/27.
tythandes, *sb. pl.* tidings, 112/142.

þ.

þan, *pron. acc.* them, 18/33.
þase, *pron.* those, 12/1.
þere, *adj.* these, 38/20.
þof(e), *conj.* though, 7/6, 33/29, 40/8.
þusgate, *adv.* in this way, thus, 20/11.

V.

venqwyste, *vb. pp.* vanquished, 94/75.
verray, *adj.* true, 45/26, 79/5, 86/87.
verraymente, *adv.* truly, 84/36.
versy, *vb. imp.* repeat verses, 40/16.
vesete, *vb. inf.* visit, 9/29.
vesettis, *vb.* 3 *sg. pr.* clothes, 90/73; vesete, *pp.* 20/20.
vgglynes, *sb.* abhorrence, detestation, 45/18.
vmbethynke, *vb. sg. imp.* think, take heed, 17/27, 26/34.
vmbythynkynge, *sb.* meditation, 17/16.
vmbylowkede, *vb. pp.* included, 7/10.
vn-bouxsomnes, *sb.* disobedience, 12/19, 24/7.
vndirlowttes, *sb.* dependants, 2/13.
vndirtane, *vb. pp.* undertaken, 55/10.
vndreghe, *adj.* impatient, 113/171.
vndrone, *sb.* the time about 9 o'clock in the morning, 43/7, 73/376.
vnhamlynes, *sb.* want of familiarity, affectation, 12/19.
vnkyndly, *adj.* unnatural, 24/6.
vnmyste, *adj.* (?) not missed, obtained, 105/255.
vnskilwyse, *adj.* unreasonable, 13/5.
vnthewes, *sb. pl.* vices, 57/1.
vntill, *prep.* unto, 2/22, 9/22, 10/7.
vppe-rysynge, *sb.* resurrection, 3/26.

W.

wakire, *adj.* watchful, 54/20, 60/15.
wakkyn, *vb. inf.* wake up, 60/16; wakyns, 3 *pl. pr.* 60/18, 19; wakenede, *pp.* 60/26.
wandes, *sb. pl.* rods, 102/171.
wandreth, *sb.* misery, distress, 11/23.
wanes, *sb. pl.* dwellings, houses, property, 98/45.
waresche, *vb.* 3 *sg. pr.* protects, cures, 25/30.
warre, *adj.* cautious, 54/20.
was, *sb.* torch, 91/89.

wate, *vb.* 1 *sg. pr.* know, 34/10; 2 *sg.
pr.* 30/32; 3 *sg. pr.* 9/3.
wathes, *sb. pl.* dangers, 11/17.
wattyr, *sb.* water, 114/15.
wawkes, *sb.* watch, dying person,
115/1.
waxande, *vb. prp.* growing, 21/32.
wayke, *adj.* weak, 55/9.
wayknes, *sb.* weakness, 41/2.
wele, *adv.* well, 3/33.
weled, *vb.* 3 *pl. pt.* chose, 105/252.
wemles, *adj.* without harm or
blemish, spotless, 20/21, 67/133.
wende, *vb. inf.* go, 3/33.
wenys, *vb.* 3 *sg. pr.* thinks, 24/11.
were, *sb.* doubt, 8/8.
werede, *vb.* 2 *sg. pt.* didst keep off,
99/56.
weryede, *vb.* 3 *pl. pt.* cursed,
103/195.
wetandly, *adv.* knowingly, 7/3,
72/314.
whanhope, *sb.* despair, 10/33.
whatekyn, *adj.* what kind of, 89/35.
wheþer so, *pron.* whoever, which-
ever, 5/2, 14/21.
wheþer-som, *adv.* wheresoever,
41/33.
whethir, *conj.* still, nevertheless,
3/16.
whethire so, *pron.* whichsoever,
11/23.
wiet(e), *vb. inf.* know, 9/23, 26/19;
2 *sg. imp.* 21/21.
wighte, *adj.* strong, vigorous, 57/26.
wilnes, *vb.* 3 *sg. pr.* desires, 12/33.
with, *prep.* by, 4/13.
witte, *sb.* knowledge, 23/34.
witterly, *adv.* surely, 60/29.
witterwyssynge, *sb.* guidance, in-
struction, 14/10.
witty, *adj.* wise, 55/21.
woddyse, *sb. pl.* woods, 114/14.
wode, *adj.* mad, 71/305.
wodnese, *sb.* madness, 114/15.

wone, *sb.* store, plenty, 102/179;
wane, 102/181.
wonn, *vb. inf.* live, dwell, 82/80;
wonne, 1 *sg. pr.* 76/44.
wonnynge, *sb.* dwelling, 64/40.
worthe, *vb. inf.* become, 61/25.
wounte, *vb.* 3 *sg. pt.* was accustomed,
48/1; *pp.* 13/20.
wreke, *vb. inf.* avenge, 12/33.
wrenkis, *sb. pl.* wiles, tricks, 55/5.
wrethe, *sb.* anger, wrath, 12/31,
107/10.
wrethe, *vb. inf.* anger, 71/292; 2 *sg.
imp.* 50/1.
wyes, *sb. pl.* men, 102/159.
wyet(e), *vb. inf.* know, 17/26, 21/23.
wyghtes, *sb. pl.* creatures, 61/35.
wyll, *adj.* wild, ignorant, self-willed,
9/35.
wyllosay, *sb.* (what) wilt-thou-say,
or, more probably an exclamation
like *walaway*, 117/52.
wyllylyere, *adv.* more readily, 60/17.
wysse, *vb. inf.* guide, teach, show,
9/35, 72/319; *sg. imp.* 97/13;
wysses, 3 *sg. pr.* 11/17.
wytes, *vb.* 3 *sg. pr.* departs, goes,
107/4.

3.

ʒelde, *vb. inf.* requite, 95/86.
ʒeme, *vb. inf.* take care of, keep, ob-
serve, 79/19; ʒemes, 3 *sg. pr.* 7/19,
11/30, 53/33.
ʒerely, *adv.* year by year, 58/24.
ʒerne, *vb. inf.* desire, 6/32; 1 *pl. pr.*
6/24, 29; ʒernes, 3 *sg. pr.* 5/30.
ʒode, *vb.* 3 *sg. pt.* went, 41/33, 99/71.
ʒolden, *vb. pp.* paid, 26/25.
ʒonge, *adj.* young, 102/183.

Y.

ynence, *prep.* anent, concerning,
against, 26/30, 34/13.
yrke, *vb. inf.* to feel dislike, 25/7.

INDEX OF NAMES.

A.
Apocalips, 101/130.
Asye, Asia, 100/101.
Atemperance, Waiter, 56/27.
Austyn, Saynt, 22/13, 36/2, 59/26.

B.
Barthilmewe, Saynte, 55/28, 32.
Bedleme, 97/7.
Bernarde, Sayne, 16/20, 31/2, 59/31.
Bowsomnes, Damsel, 52/17.

C.
Charite, Abbess, 54/4.
Contemplacione, Builder, 53/14.
Craton, 103/210.
Curtasye, Receiver of Guests, 57/10.

D.
Damesele Conande and Wysse, þat es callede Meditacyone, Storekeeper, 57/29.
Danyele, 55/12.
Dauid, 52/29.
Denyse, Saynte, 58/20.
Deuocion, Cellaress, 53/23, 56/16.
Discrecyone, Treasurer, 55/21.
Domycyane, Domitian, 100 / 111, 101/141.
Drede, Porteress, 56/35.
Drucyane, 102/153.

E.
Envye, Damsel, 61/15.
Ephesym, Ephesus, 101/144.

F.
False Demynge of Oþer, Damsel, 61/17.
Forte, Damsel, 52/35.

G.
Gabrielle, 39/3.
Gaytryge, Dan Iohn, 1/1.
Gelosye, Time-keeper, 60/14.
Gregore, Saynt, 37/7.
Gruchynge, Damsel, 61/16.

H.
Herod, 69/206.
Honeste, Mistress of the Novices, 57/5.

I.
Iewes, 68/194, 196, 69/231.
Iewry, 70/259.
Ihesu Criste, 31/1, &c.
Iob, 59/31.
Iohn, Sayn, 11/7, 14/34, 68/174.
Iourdane, 68/175.
Iubilacion, Chantress, 56/5.
Iudas, 68/193, 71/298, 304.

K.
Katerin, Saynt, 119/10.

L.
Largesse, Nurse, 57/28.
Lewte, Nurse, 57/24.
Longyous, Longinus, 119/2.
Luffe of Clennes, Maiden, 51/14.

M.
Margarete, Saynt, 119/9.
Marye, Saynte, 79/1, 84/35.
Mathewe, Sayne, 9/24.
Meditacion, Builder, 53/24.
Meditacyone, Store-keeper, 57/30.
Mekenes, Maiden, 51/19.
Meknes, Sub-prioress, 54/29.
Mercy, Almoner, 56/34.
Michaelle, 39/3.
Miserecorde, Damsel, 52/18.

N.
Nabogodhonosore, 55/13.
Nassyngton, William, 63.

O.
Olyuere, Cragge of, 120/31.
Oracion, Builder, 53/14.
Orysone, Chantress, 55/23.

P.
Pathmos, Patmos, 101/129.
Paule, Sayn, 2/12, 16/5, 40/11.

Index of Names.

Penance, Cook, 56/20.
Pete, Butler or Pittancer, 56/32, 58/32.
Pilate, 69/210, 212, 232.
Poleschesy, Store-keeper, 57/30.
Porte Latyn, 100/116.
Pouerte, Maiden, 51/20.
Predicacion, Builder, 53/13.
Pride, Damsel, 61/16.

R.
Raphaelle, 39/3.
Resone, Purveyor, 57/22.

Rewfulnes, Builder, 53/23.
Rightwynes, Maiden, 51/14.
Rome, 55/13.

S.
Salomon, 52/25.
Scrifte, Builder, 53/13.
Sobirnes, Reader, 56/29.
Sufferance, Damsel, 52/35.
Symplese, Receiver of Guests, 57/15

W.
Wysdome, Prioress, 54/22.